KENNETH COX

THE
SANCTUARY
PURE AND SIMPLE

Thank you so much for your prayers and support of the ministry. God bless you for your kindness.

Kenneth Cox

KENNETH COX

THE
SANCTUARY
PURE AND SIMPLE

3ABN
books

Kenneth Cox Ministries

Cover and Inside Layout and Design: Chrystique Neibauer | cqgraphicdesign.com
Chapter Illustrations: Jillian Vaughan Graphic Design
Cover Images: shutterstock.com and Jillian Vaughan
Copyright © 2014 by Kenneth Cox Ministries

Scripture quoted from NKJV, THOMAS NELSON

Additional copies of this book are available from:

Kenneth Cox Ministries: Call (951) 232-9822 or visit www.kennethcoxministries.org.
Write to P.O. Box 1027, Loma Linda, CA 92354

Adventist Book Centers®: Call toll-free 1-800-765-6955 or visit
www.adventistbookcenter.com.

3ABN: Call (618) 627-4651 or visit www.store.3abn.org.

3ABN Books is dedicated to bringing you the best in published materials consistent
with the mission of Three Angels Broadcasting Network. Our goal is to uplift
Jesus Christ through books, audio, and video materials by our family of 3ABN
presenters. Our in-depth Bible study guides, devotionals, biographies, and lifestyle
materials promote whole person health and the mending of broken people. For more
information, call (618) 627-4651 or visit 3ABN's Web site: www.3ABN.org.

Dedication

This book is dedicated to Jesus Christ the Lamb of
God, who, in the sanctuary service so beautifully
illustrates His marvelous gift of grace. And to
"those who follow the Lamb where He goes."
(Rev 14:4)

Table of Contents

Acknowledgments

To the work of the Holy Spirit in inspiring those who have worked on this publication. Their friendship and contribution has been invaluable. Dona Klein, Bob Hablutzel, Diane Loer, Lindi McDougal. No matter if their part was large or small, I know their motivation was their desire to see men and women come to know Jesus Christ. Thank you for the encouragement and help in the writing of this book.

Introduction

As Abraham, the father of the Jewish nation, made his way into the land of Canaan, he erected an altar at Shechem, at Bethel, and at Hebron. He understood that sacrifices offered upon these altars were a type of the Redeemer who would one day die for his sins. However, it was not until the Lord told him to offer his son Isaac as a sacrifice on mount Moriah that Abraham realized the significance of the sacrifices being offered. Christ, the true sacrifice, spoke of this experience as follows: "*Your father Abraham rejoiced to see My day, and he saw it and was glad.*" John 8:56. This was something Abraham shared with Isaac, and which was subsequently passed on to Jacob through Isaac. However, it would take more than word of mouth to communicate this great truth to the more than one million people coming out of slavery in Egypt.

To serve as an object lesson to the children of Israel, God told Moses to build a Sanctuary that would teach them the great plan of salvation. When using the word 'Sanctuary,' I am referring to the entire structure, including the court and the tabernacle. The sanctuary was a portable structure attended to by the Levites, and carried by them when Israel traveled from place to place Numbers 1:50. Everything in the life of ancient Israel revolved around the Sanctuary and the services conducted in it. It was the center of the Jewish economy and the hub of activities during their forty years of wandering in the wilderness. Fittingly, the Sanctuary was erected in the center of Israel's encampments. Three of Israel's twelve tribes camped on each of its four sides and the Levites camped immediately around it (Numbers 1:52, 53). This provided it tremendous protection.

The primary purpose of the earthly Sanctuary was to provide a place for God to dwell among His people. As God told Moses on Mount Sinai, *"And let them* [the children of Israel] *make Me a sanctuary, that I may dwell among them. According to all that I show you, that is, the pattern of the tabernacle and the pattern of all its furnishings, just so you shall make it."* Exodus 25:8-9. The earthly Sanctuary was of divine origin, for it was carefully patterned after God's true Sanctuary in heaven. Hebrews 8:1-2. Although the earthly Sanctuary was made by the hand of man, God provided Moses with a very detailed blueprint for its construction, and the construction of everything associated with it. Every component of the Sanctuary had a specific function, and was to be made exactly according to God's pattern of the heavenly Sanctuary. No guesswork or supposition was left to the mind of man, not even in the minutest detail. Every element of the Sanctuary had its place and its purpose, and nothing was to be misplaced or overlooked. This would ensure that the symbolism of the Sanctuary, which was to serve as an object lesson for the people, would typify the truths being represented. Just as God told Moses, *"let them build Me a sanctuary that I may dwell among them"* 1500 years later, the Son of God would once again dwell with mankind: *"And the Word became flesh and dwelt among us, and we beheld His glory, the glory as of the only begotten of the Father, full of grace and truth."* John 1:14. In the Sanctuary, Israel was to learn of the sacrifice the Messiah would make for their salvation. Through the Sanctuary services, they were to see the love, mercy, and character of God.

THE
SANCTUARY
PURE AND SIMPLE

CHAPTER 1

The Court

The Court

The tabernacle was surrounded by a court that was approximately 150 feet long by 75 feet wide. Exodus 27:9 describes the hangings for the court [the curtains surrounding it] as being made ". . . *of fine woven linen*". They were an impressive sight, very delicate and beautiful. The hangings on the north, south and west sides measured the same as the court, respectively. The hangings on the east side consisted of approximately 22.5 feet of fine woven linen on each side of the gate. Sixty bronze pillars with capitals of silver supported these hangings. The pillars were equidistant from one another, each pillar rested in a socket of bronze. Beautiful silver hooks and inserts secured the hangings to the pillars. Rods of equal height and equal width, covered with silver and joined with tendons resting in silver sockets, composed the rib-work for the hangings which enclosed the court (See Exodus 27:9-19).

The gate provided the entrance to the court. It was approximately 30 feet wide by 7.5 feet high. The screen for the gate opening consisted of intricate needlework of blue, purple and scarlet thread, and fine woven linen (see Exodus 27:16). All materials used in the construction of the screen blended harmoniously. The screen for the gate had four pillars and accompanying hardware to match the rest of the hangings for the Tabernacle. Inside the court and before the Tabernacle were two articles of furniture, the altar of sacrifice and the laver.

The Earth

All the work done in the court typified the work done for man's salvation on this earth. What took place within the Tabernacle was a type of what Christ is doing for us in heaven. The territory outside the court represented the world. No sacrifice was ever offered inside the Tabernacle; the offering was slain in the court. The priest then carried the blood and flesh into the Tabernacle. Only those who accepted the Lord, and followed Him, were allowed inside the court. It was there that a person would bring a lamb, confess their sins on its head, and then take its life for the remission of sins. All the services that took place in the court found their fulfillment in Christ, and what He has done for us on this earth. Thus, it was on this earth that the Lamb of God shed His blood for the forgiveness of our sins and the justification of sinners.

In Revelation 11:1-2, John explains what the court represented: *"Then I was given a reed like a measuring rod. And the angel stood, saying, "Rise and measure the temple of God, the altar, and those who worship there. But leave out the court which is outside the temple, and do not measure it, for it has been given to the Gentiles."* Measuring had to do with judgment. Bear in mind that the Sanctuary, or Temple on earth, was made after the pattern in heaven. We know this text is referring to the temple in heaven, because John wrote the book of Revelation about A.D. 90, and at that time the temple in Jerusalem had already been destroyed. *"Those who worship there"* refers to God's people, since this is a judgment picture. 1 Peter 4:17 tells us that the judgment began with God's people. When Revelation 11:2 states, *"But leave out the court which is outside the temple, and do not measure it, for it has been given to the Gentiles,"* the word "Gentiles" is the same Greek word that is used for "nations" in Revelation 11:18. It means "people of the world," or "those who do not follow God". Not measuring the court (for it has been given to the Gentiles) tells us that the wicked will be judged at a time later than the judgment of the redeemed. All the work that took place within the court was symbolic, and meets its fulfillment in the reality of God's plan of salvation.

THE
SANCTUARY
PURE AND SIMPLE

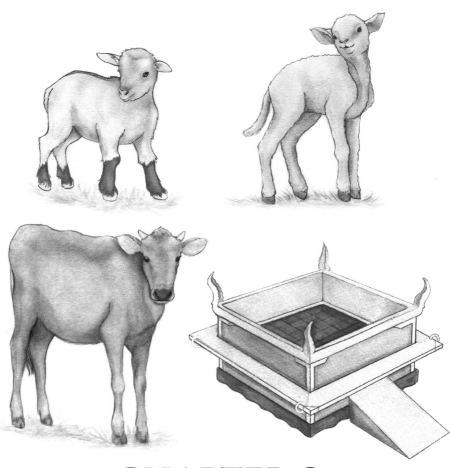

CHAPTER 2

The Altar of Sacrifice and the Lamb of God

Altar of Sacrifice

Inside the court and near its entrance was the brazen altar, referred to in Scripture as the *altar of burnt offering*. It was approximately seven and a half feet long, seven and a half feet wide, and four and a half feet high. On each corner were the "horns of the altar," representing God's forgiveness, and a place of refuge. For example, when Solomon ordered that Joab be killed, Joab fled to the tabernacle and took hold of the horns of the altar (1 Kings 2:28), believing it was a place where he could find refuge and receive forgiveness. The altar was made of shittim (acacia) wood, which was used for construction throughout the tabernacle. The altar was then completely covered with brass, which is why some Bible translations refer to it as the brazen altar. A full description of the altar is found in Exodus 27:1-8.

The Lord was also very explicit in His instructions to the Israelites concerning burnt offerings. Almost all offerings were brought to the sanctuary and offered on the altar of sacrifice. There were many different reasons for bringing an offering. The sacrificial procedure varied depending upon the reason for the sacrifice, and the type of animal being sacrificed. For example, individuals were required to bring an animal to the altar of burnt offering for the forgiveness of his or her sins. The animal could be a bull, a lamb, a goat, or even a turtledove, depending upon the person's financial circumstances, but each animal must be without spot or blemish.

Leviticus 4:1-35 describes the sin offering. When one of the common people sinned *unintentionally*, the sacrifice of a female sheep or goat was required. He or she would place their hands on the head of the sacrifice and confess their sins. The person then took a knife and cut the throat of the sacrifice, for "*. . . without shedding of blood there is no remission* of sin." Hebrews 9:22. The priest then caught the blood of the sacrifice in a basin and proceeded to the altar of sacrifice. He then dipped his finger in the blood and applied it to the horns of the altar while confessing the person's sins. The remaining blood was poured at the base of the altar (Leviticus 4:29, 30). All the fat of the sacrifice was removed, and the priest then burned the sacrifice on the altar for a sweet aroma to the Lord. The body of the sacrifice was completely consumed.

In this way, the sins of the individual vicariously passed to the priest through the blood of the animal sacrifice. By demonstrating their faith in the coming Lamb of God who would one day pay the supreme sacrifice to cleanse them from all unrighteousness, the penitent sinner now knew that his sins had been forgiven, and that they were no longer under condemnation. This sacrificial system was *the gospel in symbols*. It was God's great object lesson, used to teach the people His plan of salvation.

To read more about specific offerings, please see the Scriptures, and the following explanations:

Sin Offering — Leviticus 1:3, 4:2-35

This offering brought the penitent sinner into close contact with the Lord, since he realized he was placing his hands upon the head of the sacrifice that was being offered for his sins. Two things were required of the individual as he brought the offering: he had to understand his own sinfulness before God, and he had to desire forgiveness enough to bring the sacrifice. Since the blood of bulls and goats could not take away sin (Hebrews 10:4), the penitent must by faith see beyond the offering to the time when the Son of God would pay the supreme price for his sins. As 1 John 1:7 states, "*. . . the* *blood of Jesus Christ His Son cleanses us from all sin."* After the sacrifice had been slain, the sinner, with his own hands, was to remove all the fat from the various organs and give it to the priest to be burned on the brazen altar. Since the offering represented the spotless Lamb of God in whom there was no sin (Hebrews 4:15), and since the fat represented sin (Leviticus 16:25 and Isaiah 43:23, 24), the symbolism of sin had to be removed from the sacrifice before it could be offered. There are few things more disagreeable to smell than burning fat, but Exodus and Leviticus refer to fat being burned as a *sweet aroma* to the Lord, because sin was being separated from the sinner. The symbolism of the One the sacrifice represented is why each sacrificial animal was to be without spot or blemish as far as the human eye could detect.

Whole Burnt Offering — *Leviticus 1:2, 9:7, 14:19-20*

The burnt offering differed from the sin offering in that the whole animal was placed on the altar and wholly consumed by fire. This type of offering existed from the time of Adam and Eve, and continued through the age of the patriarchs. God's people erected altars in the various places they traveled. As the Scriptures record, the head of the family would erect an altar, and then offer a sacrifice for himself and his family for the forgiveness of sins. The altars also represented total dedication to the Lord, such as we find in the lives of Abraham, Isaac and Jacob. With the birth of the Israelite nation, God had them build a central place where the animal sacrifices were brought and offered by the priest. There were special occasions when an offering was made outside the Sanctuary, such as when David offered a sacrifice at the threshing-floor of Ornan (1 Chronicles 21:18-30), and when Elijah offered a sacrifice to God on Mt. Carmel (1 Kings 18:31-38). Each morning and evening, a lamb was to be offered as a whole burnt offering for the entire congregation. This was a time of dedicating their lives to the service of God. The admonition to us today is, *"I beseech you therefore, brethren, by the mercies of God, that you present your bodies a living sacrifice, holy, acceptable to God, which is your reasonable service."* Romans 12:1. Above all, God desires our hearts, our love: *"And to love Him with all the heart, with all the understanding, with all the soul, and with all the strength, and to love one's neighbor as oneself, is more than all the whole burnt offerings and sacrifices."* Mark 12:33.

Meat Offering — *Leviticus 2:1-15*

The word *meat* in the English languish is misleading in that it can mean food other than flesh. Such was the case with the meat offering, which was not an animal, but fruits and grains. It was offered each morning and evening along with the burnt offering, and could be brought by the poor as an offering in place of an animal. It was always seasoned with salt, and burned on the altar of sacrifice. The seasoning of salt was a reminder of God's covenant with Israel, that He would be their God, and they would be His people. He would bless them and save them if they were willing to keep His commandments, and only faith in the righteousness of the Savior to come, could make the service acceptable to Him.

Drink Offering — *Numbers 28:7-8*

A drink offering was offered to the Lord each morning and evening at the time of the burnt offering. This was a sign of the people's dedication to God, and of the renewal of their commitment to Him. Drink offerings existed before God's Sanctuary directive was given at Mt. Sinai. As Jacob entered the land of Canaan after spending twenty years with Laban,

God showed him in a dream that He would be with him and bless him. In the morning, Jacob poured out a drink offering to the Lord (Genesis 35:10-14). When three of David's mighty warriors heard him say that he wished he could have a drink of water from the well in Bethlehem, they broke through the enemy's line and brought David water from the well. Instead of drinking it, David felt it was too sacred, and poured it out on the ground as a drink offering to the Lord (1 Chronicles 11:17-19).

Trespass Offering — *Leviticus 5:15, 6:2*

Some Bible students make no difference between the sin offering and the trespass offering. The Scripture speaks primarily of two areas in which the trespass offering was used. One area was sins that involved holy things, such as the tithe, offering of the first fruits, and anything the Lord said was holy. If an individual had sinned by using such a thing to benefit himself rather than to glorify God, he was to bring a trespass offering. The other area in which the trespass offering was used was when a person had stolen something, which required restitution be made. The individual was required to restore the full amount of the item to the owner, and the priest was to declare the item's value, and then add one fifth of that value to the total. A good example of this was Zacchaeus, who not only offered a sacrifice, but restored what he had taken fourfold (Luke 19:8). The trespass offering was more complete than the sin offering, in that it also covered the *results* of sin. By His death, Christ not only satisfied the demands of the law, He also covered the results of sin by making all things new.

Peace & Freewill Offerings — *Leviticus 3, 22:21*

"Peace, peace, wonderful peace, coming down from the

Father above." How many long for this peace? Only in Christ is this peace to be found. Charles Spurgeon, the great preacher of England, said, "I looked to Christ and the dove of peace flew into my heart; I looked at the dove of peace and it flew away." Any one of the children of Israel could have assurance of this peace by bringing a peace offering to the Lord. In this offering were all the elements involved in obtaining peace. The individual would place his hands on the head of the spotless animal he had brought, confess his sins with his hands placed upon the head of the animal, and then slay it. He was then required to separate the fat from the various organs of the animal and then give it to the priest, who burned it on the altar of sacrifice. Just as the fat of the animal represented sin, the first step in obtaining peace is that we must be willing to separate ourselves from our sins by confessing them to Christ. *"If we confess our sins, He is faithful and just to forgive us our sins and to cleanse us from all unrighteousness."* 1 John 1:9.

The next step in obtaining peace is to trust in the Lord: *"Trust in the Lord with your heart and lean not to your own understanding"* Proverbs 3:5. Only with this Peace offering, and Passover offering, were the people allowed to eat the flesh of the sacrifice. Unlike the Passover offering, which was offered once a year, the peace offering could be brought anytime. The individual making the offering was instructed by God not to eat by himself, but to invite his family, his friends, and the Levite. The offering was one of thanksgiving for God's mercy and goodness, and it was to be shared with others as an object lesson of God's care for all of His people.

We often fear to trust God with the affairs of our daily lives. The result is that, after we have accepted Christ and been forgiven, we soon find ourselves troubled and perplexed by the cares of this life, and we lose the peace that Christ gave us

(John 14:27). He warns about this in Matthew 13:22, *"Now he who received seed among the thorns is he who hears the word, and the cares of this world and the deceitfulness of riches choke the word, and he becomes unfruitful."* Paul referred to the offering of peace in 1 Corinthians 15:3-4, *"For I delivered to you first of all that which I received: that Christ died for our sins according to the Scripture. And that He was buried, and that He rose again the third day according to the Scripture."* The phrase *"according to the Scripture"* means that it happened *exactly* as the Scriptures prophesied it would happen. This text has to be speaking of the Old Testament Scriptures, because the New Testament had not yet been written. The details regarding how the Peace Offering was to be cared for provided the lesson of how long Christ would be in the grave: *"And if you offer a sacrifice of a peace offering to the Lord, you shall offer it of your own free will. It shall be eaten the same day you offer it, and on the next day. And if any remains until the third day, it shall be burned in the fire. And if it is eaten at all on the third day, it is an abomination. It shall not be accepted"* Leviticus 19:5-7. Remember that the animal being sacrificed was a symbol of Christ, and His sacrificial death. (Peace came by knowing that Christ would rise on the third day,) victorious over death and the grave. He is now alive and in heaven, seated at the right hand of His father, and is ready to send light, help and peace to those who trust in Him (See Hebrews 8:1-2).

Offering the Red Heifer — *Numbers 19:2-10*

The offering of the Red Heifer was different in many ways from the other offerings. It was killed outside the camp, not in the court of the Sanctuary. Unlike the other offerings, the blood of the heifer had no contact with the Sanctuary, and was not carried into the Tabernacle. Its blood was not put on the horns of the altar of sacrifice, it was not poured out at base of the altar, it was not carried into the holy place, it was not sprinkled on the veil, and it was not placed upon the horns of the altar of incense. The heifer had to be red and, like the other animals sacrificed, without spot or blemish, for it represented the spotless Lamb of God who would offer His blood for their salvation.

The heifer was led outside the camp by the priest and elders to a valley that had never been sown or cultivated, where it was then killed. The priest took some of the blood and sprinkled it seven times towards the temple. This offering involved purification of the land and the people. The Israelites were exposed to paganism in Egypt, whose inhabitants worshiped the dead, for four hundred years. After freeing them from bondage in Egypt, God put into effect strict laws regarding how to care for the dead (Numbers 21:1-9). Any contact with a dead person or dead animal was considered a defilement. Communication with the dead was considered an abomination. The direction given the children of Israel, that "the dead know nothing," is consistent with the rest of Scripture (See Ecclesiastes 9:5 and Job 7:9-10). Israel's hope was in the sacrifice offered in the court, where the blood, which represented the death of Christ, was applied for the sins of individuals. The offering of the heifer outside the court has great symbolism. Christ was crucified outside the walls of Jerusalem, representing that He died for the sins of the whole world, and not just those of the Jewish people. Just as the sinner would come by faith and offer his sacrifice as a symbol of his acceptance of the promised Redeemer who would one day die for his sins, so today, you and I who live *after* the cross, must come to Christ in faith, believing that He died for our sins.

The Lamb of God

The concept of a sacrificial animal, representing the sacrifice that Christ would make for mankind's salvation, is consistent throughout Scripture. As far back as Abraham and Isaac, this great truth was spoken: *"My son, God will provide for Himself the lamb for a burnt offering."* Genesis 22:8. Isaiah prophesied of Christ's sacrifice in these terms, *". . . He was led as a lamb to the slaughter, and as a sheep before its shearers is silent, so He opened not His mouth"* Isaiah 53:7. Seven hundred years later, John the Baptist exclaimed as he saw Jesus approaching, *". . . Behold! The Lamb of God who takes away the sin of the world!"* John 1:29. Just as the animal sacrifice was to be without spot or blemish, Jesus, the true Lamb of God, came without sin, pure and undefiled. Peter said that mankind was redeemed *"with the precious blood of Christ, as of a lamb without blemish and without spot."* 1 Peter 1:19. We find Christ referred to as *"the Lamb"* at least 41 times in the book of Revelation alone. Therefore, when a repentant sinner brought a sacrificial lamb to the sanctuary, there was no question as to whom it represented. For a thousand years, this lesson was before the people in preparation for the coming of Jesus Christ, the *true* Lamb of God.

THE
SANCTUARY
PURE AND SIMPLE

CHAPTER 3

The Laver and Water of Life

Laver

The laver stood between the altar of sacrifice and the tabernacle. Scripture is silent concerning its measurements. It does state that it sat on a base, which made it easier to use. It was cast from bronze mirrors furnished by the women of Israel (Exodus 30:18, 38:8). Since it had to be transportable, its heavy bronze construction probably limited its size. The laver served as a wash basin for the hands and feet of the priests. This was required before entering the Holy Place, or the Most Holy Place of the tabernacle, or before offering a sacrifice on the altar. A violation of that command carried the penalty of death. Just as the Lord told Moses at the burning bush, *". . . Take your sandals off your feet, for the place where you stand is holy ground"* (Exodus 3:5), the sanctuary too, was holy, for God's presence was in the Most Holy Place. As a result, the priests were to remove their footwear before entering the tabernacle. Dust or dirt on their shoes, feet or hands would defile it. The lesson that defilement must be put away before entering the presence of God, was ever before the Israelites (Exodus 30:17-21).

Water of Life

Water was used for both physical and spiritual cleansing. As Paul wrote regarding the church, *"that He might sanctify and cleanse her with the washing of water by the word."* Ephesians 5:26. God uses water as a symbol for the Holy Spirit, for the Word of God, and for the gift of eternal life. Jesus gave the invitation to the woman at Jacob's well, *"If you knew the gift of God, and who it is who says to you, 'Give Me a drink,' you would have asked Him, and He would have given you living water."* John 4:10. Throughout the ages, men have searched for something to satisfy their souls. Only He who is the Water of Life can quench the thirst in our hearts. As Jesus told the woman, *"Whoever drinks of this [physical] water will thirst again."* John 4:13. Nothing this world has to offer, including education, fame, or money, fills that need; the individual remains thirsty. In contrast, when we drink of the spiritual water Christ offers us, we will never thirst again. Speaking of the Holy Spirit, Jesus said, *"He who believes in Me, as the Scripture has said, out of his heart will flow rivers of living water." But this He spoke concerning the Spirit . . ."* John 7:38-39. The book of Revelation ends by inviting everyone to receive this wonderful gift: *"And the Spirit and the bride say, "Come!" And let him who hears say, "Come!" And let him who thirsts come. Whoever desires, let him take the water of life freely."* Revelation 22:17.

Christ instituted a new form of cleansing on the evening of the Lord's Supper. When he came to Peter to wash his feet, Peter objected by saying, *"You shall never wash my feet!"* Jesus answered him, *"If I do not wash you, you have no part with Me."* Simon Peter said to Him, *"Lord, not my feet only, but also my hands and my head!"* John 13:8, 9.

Christ's reply explained the meaning of washing their feet: *" 'He who is bathed needs only to wash his feet, but is completely clean; and you are clean, but not all of you'. For He knew who would betray Him; therefore He said, 'You are not all clean' "* John 13:10, 11. When we accept Christ and are baptized, from a spiritual standpoint, we have been bathed. The blood of Jesus Christ washes all our sins away, and in the eyes of God, we are completely clean. However, as we walk daily with Christ, we sometimes stumble and get dust on our feet. Christ gave the ordinance of foot washing as an object lesson. If we sin, we do not need to be re-baptized. As is represented in the imagery of the Lord's Supper, we can have our feet spiritually washed by confessing our sins to God. When we do, we know that our sins are forgiven, and that we are cleansed through the body and the blood of Christ (1 John 1:9). Christ is the Water of Life, and by reaching out to Him in faith, this Living Water makes us spotless and clean.

THE
SANCTUARY
PURE AND SIMPLE

CHAPTER 4

Priesthood and the Levites

The Levites

From the beginning, God said that the head of the household was the priest, and that he was responsible for the spiritual life of the family. The first born of a household was consecrated to God. They were His. The tribe of Levi was the only tribe that remained true to God by not worshiping the golden calf at Mt. Sinai. In return, the Lord transferred the privileges and duties of the firstborn to them. They received the honor of ministering for Him (See Numbers 3:12). Even then, the firstborn of each family had to be redeemed with a sacrifice because they belonged to God. (See Exodus 34:20).

The Levites camped closest to the Sanctuary, and had the responsibility of caring for it. They were divided into four groups: Aaron and his descendents, the Gershonites, the Kohathites and the Merarites. Each group was responsible for different duties in caring for, and in moving, the tabernacle. Each time the Israelites moved to a new location during their wilderness travels, Aaron and his sons placed a special covering over each piece of furniture in the Sanctuary. Then the other divisions of Levites would carry the various articles of the Sanctuary to the next location.

The tribe of Levi received no inheritance in the land of Canaan. They were to spend their time ministering to the people and caring for the Sanctuary. The tithe was their means of support.

144,000

The Bible speaks of another group of people who will be given responsibility similar to that of the Levites. *"Then I looked, and behold, a Lamb standing on Mount Zion, and with Him one hundred and forty-four thousand, having His Father's name written on their foreheads. . . . These are the ones who follow the Lamb wherever He goes. These were redeemed from among men, being firstfruits to God and to the Lamb"* Revelation 14:1, 4. Just as the Levites had been chosen by God to replace the firstborn of each family, and to give themselves to ministry in the Sanctuary, so the 144,000 are the firstfruits, and will follow the Lamb wherever He goes.

The Priesthood

As long as the Sanctuary functioned as the place where the children of Israel were to take their sacrifices, the priesthood was to be confined to the household of Aaron, and was not to be transferred to any other family in the tribe of Levi. Exodus 29 records a special anointing service to set them apart from the rest of the Levites. Only the priest could minister in the tabernacle. He alone could handle the furniture, or offer a sacrifice to God. (See Numbers 18:1-7).

Two kings experienced the ramifications of going contrary to God's instructions concerning the duties of the priests. King Saul disregarded the Lord's instructions, offered a sacrifice, and was consequently rejected by God (See 1 Samuel 13). King Uzziah of Judah *". . . transgressed against the Lord his God by entering the temple of the Lord to burn incense on the altar of incense"* (2 Chronicles 26:16). When opposed by the priests, he became furious, and during his fit of anger he contracted leprosy. (2 Chronicles 26:16-21). God's laws concerning the duties of the priests were enforced from generation to generation.

White linen clothing clearly identified the priests. Their trousers came down to the knees, and were covered by a long-sleeved tunic which reached the ankles. A turban of white linen covered their head. Their clothing represented the Lord's desire that they be pure, holy and spotless. They were to be an example for the people, a living representation of the righteous character of God. The priests provided teaching, counsel, blessings and judgment. Therefore, through them the people were to get a glimpse of the kingdom of God.

God's People

God has promised that all of His people will be priests: *"and has made us kings and priests to His God and Father, to Him be glory and dominion forever and ever. Amen."* Revelation 1:6. God gave the priesthood to Aaron and his descendents for them to serve in a close relationship with Him. Peter talks about all of God's people having this same close relationship with Him: *"But you are a chosen generation, a royal priesthood, a holy nation, His own special people, that you may proclaim the praises of Him who called you out of darkness into His marvelous light."* 1 Peter 2:9. Throughout the ceaseless ages of eternity, God's people will serve Him in the temple in heaven.

High Priest

The High Priest was dressed distinctly differently than the other priests. The Scripture states, *"And you shall make holy garments for Aaron your brother, for glory and for beauty."* Exodus 28:2. Aaron wore knee-length white linen trousers, and a long-sleeved embroidered tunic from neck to feet. This was covered with a blue sleeveless robe. The lower hem of the tunic was fringed with small bells of gold alternating with pomegranates of blue, purple and scarlet. The ephod was placed over the tunic. It was a vest or apron richly embroidered with blue, purple, scarlet and gold. An embroidered sash of blue, purple and scarlet matching the ephod was placed around the priest's waist. An onyx stone was placed on each shoulder of the ephod, which was inscribed with the names of the tribes of Israel. (See Exodus 28:9-14). The breastplate hung from the shoulder straps of the ephod on the front of the High Priest. It was doubled into about a nine inch square, forming a pouch which was held together by golden rings fastened to golden chains, which were fastened to the shoulder straps of the ephod. On the front of the breastplate, were three rows consisting of four precious stones per row, and on each of the twelve stones was inscribed the name of one of the tribes of Israel. Revelation 21:19-20, describes the same twelve stones as forming the foundation of the wall of the New Jerusalem, which in color, makes up the colors of the rainbow. Inside the breastplate were the Urim and Thummim, which the High Priest carried over his heart, and which God used to give direction to the Children of Israel. (See Exodus 28:15-30). A fine linen turban with a golden plate, on which was engraved "Holiness To The Lord," was placed on his head. (See Exodus 28:36-38).

Jesus Christ

The book of Hebrews contains numerous texts which state that Christ is the High Priest. For example, Hebrews 6:20 states, "... *even Jesus, having become High Priest forever according to the order of Melchizedek.*" The reason Christ is High Priest after the order of Melchizedek is that Melchizedek was a king priest: "*For this Melchizedek, king of Salem, priest of the Most High God, who met Abraham returning from the slaughter of the kings and blessed him.*" (Hebrews 7:1.) Christ is the King of kings and Lord of lords, as well as being the High Priest who alone could go in before the God of the universe and minister in behalf of His people. When Jesus Christ ascended to heaven, He went as our High Priest, not to offer a lamb as a sacrifice, but to offer Himself. "*Not with the blood of goats and calves, but with His own blood He entered the Most Holy Place once for all, having obtained eternal redemption."* Hebrews 9:12. We can come boldly to the throne of grace, because the true Lamb of God is there to present His precious blood to His Father on our behalf.

THE
SANCTUARY
PURE AND SIMPLE

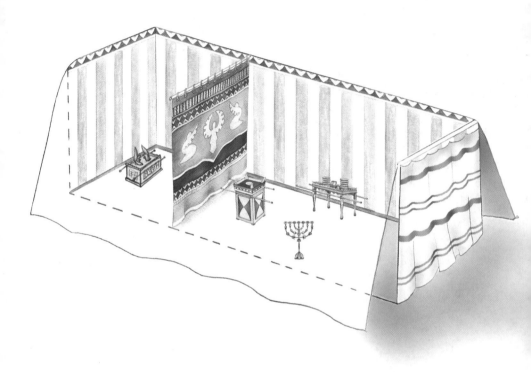

CHAPTER 5

Tabernacle

Tabernacle

For a portable building, the tabernacle was stunningly beautiful. It was erected in the middle of the camp of Israel, with the closest tent being two-thirds of a mile away. The walls of the tabernacle were 15 feet high, which was twice as high as the hangings around the court. Made of wood from the Acacia tree, each board of the tabernacle was dimensionally identical, 15 feet in length, 30 inches wide, and 3 inches thick. Each board was completely overlaid with gold. The wall on the north and south was composed of 20 boards set upright, side by side, in two sockets of silver held firmly by pillars and connecting bars overlaid with gold. The building was approximately 50 feet long and 15 feet wide. The ceiling consisted of four layers. The first layer was made of four sets of curtains held together by loops of blue yarn, and secured with clasps of gold. The curtain material was fine twine linen in colors of blue, purple and scarlet, with threads of silver and gold embroidered into pictures of angels. The tabernacle was protected from the elements by three additional coverings; the first consisted of goats hair, the second of rams skins dyed red, and lastly was the outer, visible covering of dark brown, coarse-looking badger skin, which hung down to the ground.

Christ's Character

Outwardly, the tabernacle was not at all attractive. To the casual observer it would not be considered beautiful or appealing, especially considering the materials and workmanship. How forcibly comes the lesson Christ taught, *"Woe to you, scribes and Pharisees, hypocrites! For you are like whitewashed tombs which indeed appear beautiful outwardly, but inside are full of dead men's bones and all uncleanness. Even so you also outwardly appear righteous to men, but inside you are full of hypocrisy and lawlessness."* Matthew 23:27-28. Although the outward skin which covered the tabernacle was undesirable to the eye, the objects within were beautiful, and wonderful to look upon. Isaiah gives us a look at the life of Christ: *"He shall grow up before Him as a tender plant, and as a root out of dry ground. He has no form or comeliness; and when we see Him, there is no beauty that we should desire Him. He is despised and rejected by men, a Man of sorrows and acquainted with grief. And we hid, as it were, our faces from Him; He was despised, and we did not esteem Him"* Isaiah 53:2-3. Yet, how beautiful was Jesus' character, altogether lovely. In Him was found no unkindness, hatefulness, wickedness, or spitefulness, so much so that He could say, *". . . for the ruler of this world is coming, and he has nothing in Me."* John 14:30. Instead, inside were love, joy, peace, longsuffering, kindness, goodness, faithfulness, gentleness, and self-control, all the fruits of the Spirit. This is what attracted people to Him. No matter what our condition in life, be it poor, disfigured or outwardly unattractive, it is no reason for us not to be lovely inside. If we surrender our lives to Christ, the Holy Spirit will bring about those changes in us.

THE
SANCTUARY
PURE AND SIMPLE

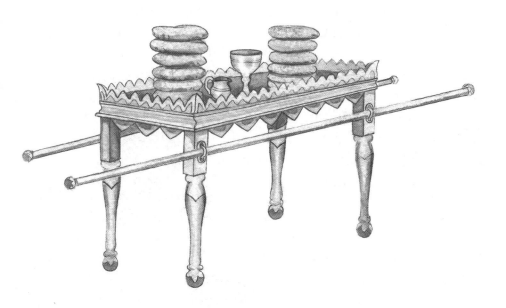

CHAPTER 6

The Golden Table of Showbread

Table of Showbread — Exodus 25:23-30, 37:10-16

As we cross the threshold of the tabernacle we enter the holy place, in which the priests ministered daily. This first of the tabernacle's two compartments, contained three pieces of furniture. On the right and to the north is the table of showbread, which is approximately 38 inches long, 18 inches wide and 27 inches high, with *". . . a molding of gold all around it"* Exodus 37:11. Around the top is a border approximately four inches high, with *". . . a crown of gold for the border thereof round about"* Exodus 37:12, KJV, which prevented any bread from falling from the table. The table, its four legs and its carrying poles, were made of acacia wood that were completely overlaid with gold. Four rings of gold were placed on the four corners of the table, into which the staves were inserted for carrying it. (See Exodus 25:23-28). The utensils of the table, *". . . its dishes, its cups, its bowls, and its pitchers for pouring"* (Exodus 37:16) were made of pure gold. The Lord told Moses, *"You shall bring in the table and arrange the things that are to be set in order on it ..."* Exodus 40:4.

The Scripture refers to the bread as *"showbread"*, *"bread of the Presence"* see Exodus 25:30 & 35:13, ESV, and *"continual showbread."* (See 2 Chronicles 2:4). because, *". . . you shall set the showbread on the table before Me always"* (Exodus 25:30). The Levites took 12 freshly baked cakes to the High Priest each Sabbath morning, and he set them on the table in two piles of six cakes each. A golden cup of pure frankincense was placed on each pile.(See Josephus Ant. 3:10, section 7). When the bread was a week old it was removed and given to the priests for food, but it was only to be eaten in a holy place. (See Leviticus 24:9). The frankincense was burned on the golden altar, and any leftover bread was burned.

Christ is the Bread of Life

The twelve cakes of bread on the table of showbread were a symbolic reminder to the twelve tribes of Israel, and that God was the provider of both their physical and spiritual food. He fed them for forty years in the wilderness. Manna was their *physical* food, and the Sanctuary services were their *spiritual* food. This was a reminder to the following generations that we must eat not only physically, but also spiritually, each day. Christ made this very clear when He said, *"This is the bread which comes down from heaven, that one may eat of it and not die. I am the living bread which came down from heaven. If anyone eats of this bread, he will live forever; and the bread that I shall give is My flesh, which I shall give for the life of the world."* John 6:50-51.

We must eat spiritually each day in order to grow spiritually and to have eternal life. Christ gave us the Lord's Supper as a reminder, *"For as often as you eat this bread and drink this cup, you proclaim the Lord's death till He comes"* 1 Corinthians 11:26. There are those who say they are followers of the Lord Jesus Christ, yet they can't quote any Scripture and they don't know the names or locations of any of the books in the Bible. Spiritually, they are emaciated, nothing but skin and bones. Eating spiritually has great reward. *"To him who overcomes I will give to eat from the tree of life, which is in the midst of the Paradise of God"* Revelation 2:7.

THE
SANCTUARY
PURE AND SIMPLE

CHAPTER 7

The Golden Lampstand

Golden Lampstand — *Exodus 25:31-40, 37:17-24*

The second piece of furniture in the tabernacle was the glorious golden lampstand. It was located on the south wall, and it was the only source of light in the holy place. The lampstand provided fuel for its seven lamps. The Jewish Tradition of lighting menorahs at Hanukkah comes from the use of the seven golden lamps in the tabernacle. It is hard to imagine how it could have been created, yet it was made from one solid, beaten piece of gold. Although the Bible does not give its size, it is estimated to have been five feet high and three and a half feet wide. The Bible does state that it was to be made *"of a talent of pure gold . . . with all its utensils"* Exodus 37:24. As a result, it would have weighed about 94.8 pounds. In today's market, that amount of gold would be worth over two million dollars.

The golden lampstand within the holy place of the ancient tabernacle was a work of extraordinary beauty. It consisted of three main parts: the base, the shaft, and the branches. From the base, a vertical shaft arose, and from each side of the shaft there were three branches which curved outward and upward. (See Exodus 25:31-35). These six branches and the center shaft each ended in a cup that was made in the form of an open almond flower. Oil lamps were placed inside the open petals of the flowers. The branches were skillfully decorated with the same open almond blossom design, with three on each branch and four on the center shaft. The oil in the seven lamps was checked twice each day, and the flax or linen wicks were trimmed so that the fire in the lamps would never go out.

Christ is the Light to the World

The Scripture repeatedly refers to Jesus as the Light, *"This man came for a witness, to bear witness of the Light, that all through him might believe. He was not that Light, but was sent to bear witness of that Light. That was the true Light which gives light to every man coming into the world."* John 1:7-9. *"In Him was life, and the life was the light of men."* John 1:4. A major change takes place when a person accepts Christ. Whereas, before, he was blinded in darkness, now he can see. Things he never understood before become clear. The promise is given, . . . *"I am the light of the world. He who follows Me shall not walk in darkness, but have the light of life."* John 8:12. This Light has shown in the hearts of millions of people throughout the world. It will never go out, but will shine brighter and brighter until that great day of His return.

Jesus spoke concerning our responsibility after we accept Him as the light of our life: *"You are the light of the world. A city that is set on a hill cannot be hidden. Nor do they light a lamp and put it under a basket, but on a lampstand, and it gives light to all who are in the house. Let your light so shine before men, that they may see your good works and glorify your Father in heaven"* Matthew 5:14-16. The Holy Spirit is the oil that causes the light to burn. Christ is the One who lights the lamp, and you and I are to make sure that we don't run out of oil. We replenish our oil by taking time each day to commune with the Lord through prayer, and through reading and following His Word. As we do so, Christ will take care of trimming the wick so that the light will shine ever brighter.

THE
SANCTUARY
PURE AND SIMPLE

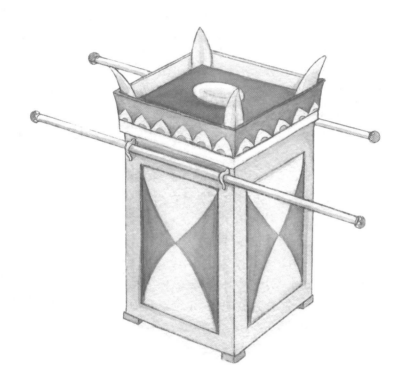

CHAPTER 8

The Golden Altar of Incense

Altar of Incense — *Exodus 30:1-5, 37:25-28*

The altar of incense was placed in the holy place in front of the veil which separated the holy place from the Most Holy Place. It was about 3 feet tall and 18 inches square, and was made of acacia wood completely overlaid with gold. *"Its horns were of one piece with it"* Exodus 37:25. *". . . He (Bezalel) also made for it a molding of gold all around it. He made two rings of gold for it under its molding, by its two corners on both sides, as holders for the poles with which to bear it. And he made the poles of acacia wood, and overlaid them with gold"* Exodus 37:26-28.

Incense was the symbol of prayer. (See Psalm 141:1-2 and Revelation 5:8; 8:3-4), and it was burned every morning and evening on this altar. In this daily act of devotion, the priest came closer to God than during any of his other duties in the holy place. The height of the veil ensured that the incense from the altar of incense filled both sections of the tabernacle. It also permitted the Shekinah Glory of the mercy seat to be partially visible from the holy place, while simultaneously obstructing any view into the Most Holy Place from the camp. This offering of incense each morning and evening was a time of worship for the Jewish people. As the incense ascended mingled with their prayers, they looked in faith toward the mercy seat, which they could not literally see.

Time of Worship

In like manner to the people of ancient Israel, we today, must look in faith to Christ, who we have not literally seen. We must have confidence in His intercession before God in our behalf, offering His life and death as atonement for our sins (Hebrews 9:24). The services performed each morning and evening at the golden altar of incense are an example to us, emphasizing the importance of beginning and ending each day with worship.

The entrance of the tabernacle always faced east. As a result, when the people were worshiping they faced west, toward the ark and the mercy seat. The Egyptians worshiped facing the rising sun in the east, and since the children of Israel spent four hundred and thirty years as slaves in Egypt, (Exodus 12:40), this method of worship had been commonplace among the Israelites. The Scripture explains God's abhorrence of sun worship. *"Then He said to me, 'Have you seen this, O son of man? Turn again, you will see greater abominations than these.' So He brought me into the inner court of the Lord's house; and there, at the door of the temple of the Lord, between the porch and the altar, were about twenty-five men with their backs toward the temple of the Lord and their faces toward the east, and they were worshiping the sun toward the east"* Ezekiel 8:15-16. God's instructions regarding the placement of the tabernacle's entrance, and its furnishings, required His people to turn their backs on this sinful practice. This trend continues today, with much of the world worshiping on *Sun*-day, and ignoring God's Sabbath day. Familiarity with sin always makes it appear to be less sinful. However, God always has a better plan.

"If you turn away your foot from the Sabbath,
From doing your pleasure on My holy day,
    And call the Sabbath a delight,
    The holy day of the Lord honorable,
    And shall honor Him, not doing your own ways,
    Nor finding your own pleasure,
    Nor speaking your own words,
    Then you shall delight yourself in the Lord;
    And I will cause you to ride on the high hills of the earth,

And feed you with the heritage of Jacob your father.
The mouth of the Lord has spoken" (Isaiah 58:13-14).

THE
SANCTUARY
PURE AND SIMPLE

CHAPTER 9

Veils

Veils

The tabernacle was divided into two compartments: the Holy Place, which occupied two thirds of the tabernacle, and the Most Holy Place, which filled the other third. The tabernacle had two veils, one at the entrance, and another, which separated the two compartments. The veil at the entrance of the tabernacle was fifteen feet wide, and fifteen feet high. Five pillars of acacia wood and their hooks, both of which were overlaid with gold, supported the veil. They were assembled with capitals and rings overlaid with gold, and with five sockets of bronze. (See Exodus 36:38). The veil was, "*. . . of blue, purple, and scarlet thread, and fine woven linen, made by a weaver.*" Exodus 36:37. The entire scene had a very striking effect upon the people when they entered the court. It was a reminder that the God of heaven and earth dwelt inside the tabernacle.

Of all the designs and colors in the Sanctuary, nothing compared to the richness and beauty of the veil which separated the Holy Place from the Most Holy Place. The veil was fifteen feet wide. Its height allowed the incense from the altar of incense to fill both sections of the tabernacle, and permitted the Shekinah Glory from the mercy seat to be partially visible from the holy place. This curtain of fine woven linen was the thickest and most costly of the two veils in the tabernacle, and its colors of blue, purple and scarlet were deeper and brighter than the veil at the entrance. It was spectacularly "*. . . woven with an artistic design of cherubim*" (Exodus 26:31), which represented the angelic host around the throne of God. The only person allowed by God to part this veil and enter the Most Holy Place was the high priest, and he was only allowed to do so once each year, on the Day of Atonement.

Christ's Atonement

This veil was miraculously torn from top to bottom when Jesus died (See Matthew 27:51), symbolizing that all the sacrifices and offerings had come to an end, for the true Lamb of God had *"died once for all."* (See Hebrews 9:14). The way into the Most Holy Place was now wide open. Man could now approach the throne of God in a new way. Jesus spoke about this when He said, *"I am the door. If anyone enters by Me, he will be saved, and will go in and out and find pasture."* John 10:9. The blood of sheep and goats could not make atonement for man's sins (See Hebrews 9:12 and 10:4). John mentions this door in the book of Revelation. *". . . These things says He who is holy, He who is true, 'He who has the key of David, He who opens and no one shuts, and shuts and no one opens' "* Revelation 3:7. The partition that separated us from the mercy seat of God was removed by the death of His Son. It is now possible for us to *". . . come boldly to the throne of grace, that we may obtain mercy and find grace to help in time of need."* Hebrews 4:16.

THE
SANCTUARY
PURE AND SIMPLE

CHAPTER 10

The Most Holy Place

Holy of Holies

God dwelt in the Most Holy Place. It was a cube, 15 feet in length, breadth and height. It contained only one article of furniture; the Ark of God, the top of which was the mercy seat. Above the mercy seat was the Shekinah Glory, the very presence of God, with a cherub on each side. The high priest entered into God's presence here once each year, on the Day of Atonement. God mandated that he be both physically and spiritually clean before entering the Holy of Holies. After bathing, he donned ". . . *the holy linen tunic and the linen trousers on his body; he shall be girded with a linen sash, and with the linen turban he shall be attired. These are holy garments*" Leviticus 16:4. These were garments of humility, for he was going before the Lord to receive cleansing for his own sins. He then took a bullock and offered it as a sacrifice for both his sins, and the sins of his family. (See Leviticus 16:6). He made his way into the Most Holy Place, sprinkling the blood of the sacrifice onto the mercy seat, and seven times before it. (See Leviticus 16:14). He was now cleansed, free from sin, and able to mediate on behalf of others.

God's Throne

The concept of a cube is used other places in Scripture in describing God's throne room. When Solomon built the temple in Jerusalem, the dimensions of the Holy of Holies were as follows: "*Then he built the twenty-cubit room at the rear of the temple, from floor to ceiling, with cedar boards; he built it inside as the inner sanctuary, as the Most Holy Place*" 1 Kings 6:16. Twenty cubits is about 30 feet. Therefore, the Most Holy Place in Solomon's temple was approximately a 30-foot cube. Following the destruction of Solomon's temple, God gave the Jewish people instructions for its rebuilding in a vision given to the prophet Ezekiel. *"He measured the length, twenty cubits; and the width, twenty cubits, beyond the sanctuary; and he said to me, 'This is the Most Holy Place'"* Ezekiel 41:4.

The book of Revelation describes the New Jerusalem as a cube. *"The city is laid out as a square; its length is as great as its breadth. And he measured the city with the reed: twelve thousand furlongs. Its length, breadth, and height are equal"* Revelation 21:16. Just as God's heavenly throne is in the New Jerusalem, His earthly throne was in the Most Holy Place of both the wilderness tabernacle, and of Solomon's temple. These were all perfect cubes which denoted God's complete, chosen church.

The sprinkling of blood in the Most Holy Place has great significance for us today; *"Not that He should offer Himself often, as the high priest enters the Most Holy Place every year with blood of another —"* Hebrews 9:25. *"And as it is appointed for men to die once, but after this the judgment, so Christ was offered once to bear the sins of many."* Hebrews 9:27-28.

THE
SANCTUARY
PURE AND SIMPLE

CHAPTER 11

Ark of the Covenant

Ark of the Covenant

The only piece of furniture in the Most Holy Place was the ark. Like all the other furniture in the tabernacle, it was made of acacia wood. It was about 45 inches long and 27 inches in both width and height, and it was completely overlaid with gold inside and out. Around the top was a most beautiful crown of gold. *"And he cast for it four rings of gold to be set in its four corners: two rings on one side, and two rings on the other side of it. He made poles of acacia wood, and overlaid them with gold. And he put the poles into the rings at the sides of the ark, to bear the ark."* Exodus 37:3-6. These staves were always to remain in the rings (See Exodus 25:15).

The ark was a chest or coffer that contained three items: God's Ten Commandment law on tables of stone, Aaron's rod that budded, and the golden pot of manna (See Hebrews 9:4). The mercy seat was *". . . on top of the ark."* Exodus 25:21. Standing upon each end of the mercy seat was a golden angel (Cherubim). *". . . He made the cherubim at the two ends of one piece with the mercy seat."* Exodus 37:8-9.

Above the mercy seat is where God's presence was manifested in what was called the *Shekinah Glory, "You shall put the mercy seat on top of the ark, and in the ark you shall put the Testimony that I will give you. And there I will meet with you, and I will speak with you from above the mercy seat, from between the two cherubim which are on the ark of the Testimony . . ."* Exodus 25:21-22. Without a doubt, when the high priest parted the veil and came into the Holy of Holies, he felt a real sense of being in the very presence of God as he stood before the ark. What the ark represented contains a very valuable lesson for each one of us.

Character

God desired to teach the people that His entire kingdom was built on the fact that He is righteous, and that His people must also be righteous. Christ's righteousness is what the life of the Christian is to emulate. There is a prophetic message in the book of Psalms that explains how Christ's life was an example of how God wants us to live; *"Sacrifice and offering You did not desire; my ears You have opened. Burnt offering and sin offering You did not require. Then I said, 'Behold, I come; In the scroll of the book it is written of me. I delight to do Your will, O my God, and Your law is within my heart.'"* Psalm 40:6-8. The apostle Paul explains, *"Therefore, when He came into the world, He said: 'Sacrifice and offering You did not desire, but a body You have prepared for Me. In burnt offerings and sacrifices for sin you had no pleasure'. Then I said, 'Behold, I have come — In the volume of the book it is written of Me — to do Your will, O God.'"* Hebrews 10:5-7. Jesus Christ fulfilled this prophecy. Placed within His heart was the Law of God. It was His character of love, and His delight to live in accordance with its precepts. Placed within the ark was the Law of God, which was to be the delight of His people. Just as the ancient Israelites had to follow it by faith because they were not allowed to see the ark, so we today, must follow by faith, that which we cannot see.

The Law or Testimony

The law was placed inside the ark because it is the foundation of God's government, the very transcript of His character of love. The Scripture uses different terms for God's law: the Ten Commandments, the Testimony, or the Covenant.

"And when He had made an end of speaking with him on Mount Sinai, He gave Moses two tablets of the <u>Testimony</u>, tablets of stone, written with the finger of God" Exodus 31:18.

"And He wrote on the tablets according to the first writing, the Ten Commandments, *which the Lord had spoken to you in the mountain from the midst of the fire in the day of the assembly; and the Lord gave them to me. Then I turned and came down from the mountain, and put the tablets in the ark which I had made; and there they are, just as the Lord commanded me."* Deuteronomy 10:4-5.

"Now it was so, when Moses came down from Mount Sinai (and the two tablets of the Testimony *were in Moses' hand when he came down from the mountain) . . ."* Exodus 34:29.

"And you shall put into the ark the Testimony *which I will give you."* Exodus 25:16.

"So He declared to you His covenant which He commanded you to perform, the Ten Commandments; *and He wrote them on two tablets of stone."* Deuteronomy 4:13.

"When I went up into the mountain to receive the tablets of stone, the tablets of the covenant *which the Lord made with you,"* Deuteronomy 9:9.

"And there I have made a place for the ark, in which is the covenant *of the Lord which He made with our fathers, when He brought them out of the land of Egypt."* 1 Kings 8:21.

Witness of the true God

The Scripture refers to the ark as *"the ark of the testimony"*, *"the ark of the covenant"* or *"the ark of the Lord"* because it contained God's law. The word *testimony* in Hebrew means evidence, proof or witness. The law of God, that is, the Ten Commandments or Decalogue, is a witness, evidence and proof that He is the true God. It testifies of His mighty power and authority as the Creator, the only God of the universe.

The dictionary describes a covenant as an agreement between two or more persons to do or to not do something specified. Therefore, the first four commandments set forth instructions concerning humankind's relationship with God. The last six commandments of the covenant outline humankind's relationship to one another. A synonym for covenant is contract. The Ten Commandments are God's contract with us that He will be our God if we will be His people.

The Lord explained it to Jeremiah as follows: "*But this is what I commanded them, saying, 'Obey My voice, and I will be your God, and you shall be My people. And walk in all the ways that I have commanded you, that it may be well with you.'*" Jeremiah 7:23.

The Manna and Aaron's Rod that Budded

A golden pot of manna was placed inside the ark with the Ten Commandments. "*Then the Lord said to Moses, 'Behold, I will rain bread from heaven for you. And the people shall go out and gather a certain quota every day, that I may test them, whether they will walk in My law or not. And it shall be on the sixth day that they shall prepare what they bring in, and it shall be twice as much as they gather daily'* " Exodus 16:4-5. Manna was a small round substance, as fine as frost. The word simply means, "*What is it?*" God fed Israel with manna for forty years in the wilderness, but it ceased to fall when they arrived at Gilgal, after crossing the Jordan. (See Joshua 5:12).

Aaron's rod that budded was also placed inside the ark with the Ten Commandments. Korah, Dathan and Abiram decided they should be in charge instead of Moses. "*They gathered together against Moses and Aaron, and said to them, "You take too much upon yourselves, for all the congregation is holy, every* one of them, and the Lord is among them. *Why then do you exalt yourselves above the assembly of the Lord?"* Numbers 16:3. They told the people that they were all priests, not just the tribe of Levi, and that God spoke to them just as much as He did to Aaron and Moses. To settle this question, *". . . the Lord spoke to Moses, saying: 'Speak to the children of Israel, and get from them a rod from each father's house, all their leaders according to their fathers' houses—twelve rods. Write each man's name on his rod. And you shall write Aaron's name on the rod of Levi . . ."* Numbers 17:1-3. Moses took the twelve rods and placed them before the Lord in the tabernacle. When Moses went into the tabernacle the next day, Aaron's rod had budded, blossomed and produced ripe almonds.

Letting God be God

As with the Ten Commandments, the golden pot of manna and Aaron's rod that budded were a witness of God's power and might to coming generations. The golden pot of manna was placed in the ark as a memorial of God's providential care of Israel, and a reminder to the Israelites of their dependence upon God. Aaron's rod that budded was placed in the ark as a memorial of the lawful priesthood, and as a reminder of who is in charge.

God demonstrated His miraculous power by supplying manna for the Israelites for 40 years in the middle of the Sinai dessert, where they would have starved to death without it. God provided only a daily portion in order to teach them their total dependence upon Him. Today, how often we forget that it is God who provides all. Imagine how long we would survive if the sun no longer shone, the rain ceased, or our supply of oxygen disappeared.

The same is true concerning our spiritual need. Jesus said, *"I am the living bread which came down from heaven. If anyone eats of this bread, he will live forever; and the bread that I shall give is My flesh, which I shall give for the life of the world."* John 6:51. Each of us needs to eat from the Word of God daily in order to prevent spiritual malnutrition.

Today, much emphasis is placed on our own ability, and more often than not, there is a, "I can handle this myself," attitude. Many have forgotten that the Lord is in charge. Aaron's rod was a sign for ancient Israel, and for coming generations, that finite man must let God, who alone sees the end from the beginning, lead. *"Trust in the Lord with all your heart, and lean not on your own understanding; In all your ways acknowledge Him, and He shall direct your paths."* Proverbs 3:5-6.

The Mercy Seat

The mercy seat was about 45 inches long and 27 inches wide. It was placed, *"... on top of the ark."* Exodus 25:21. At each end of the mercy seat were two golden cherubim. *"And you shall make two cherubim of gold; of hammered work you shall make them at the two ends of the mercy seat. Make one cherub at one end, and the other cherub at the other end; you shall make the cherubim at the two ends of it of one piece with the mercy seat"* Exodus 25:18-19. The two cherubim and the mercy seat were made of one piece of gold. *"And the cherubim shall stretch out their wings above, covering the mercy seat with their wings, and they shall face one another; the faces of the cherubim shall be toward the mercy seat."* Exodus 25:20. Above the mercy seat and between the two cherubim was the Shekinah Glory, where the very presence of God dwelt. *"And there I will meet with you, and I will speak with you from above the mercy seat, from between the two cherubim, which are on the ark of the Testimony, about everything which I will give you in commandment to the children of Israel."* Exodus 25:22. It is significant that the mercy seat was above the law, which was placed within the ark. The Scripture is limited in its literal description of the cherubim and the mercy seat. Paul explains that God will provide us with the details at some point in the future: *"And above it were the cherubim of glory overshadowing the mercy seat. Of these things we cannot now speak in detail."* Hebrews 9:5.

Righteousness and Mercy

The Ten Commandment law is God's standard of righteousness. It will never change, for it is the perfect transcript of God's perfect character of selfless love, which will never change. *"For assuredly, I say to you, till heaven and earth pass away, one jot or one tittle will by no means pass from the law till all is fulfilled."* Matthew 5:18. For a mere human being to change God's law, they would have to be greater than God. All laws require a penalty if broken. Sin is the transgression of the law, and *"The wages of sin is death . . ."* Romans 6:23.

Paul explains how Jesus Christ paid the penalty for the sins of all mankind: *"being justified freely by His grace through the redemption that is in Christ Jesus, whom God set forth as a propitiation by His blood, through faith, to demonstrate His righteousness, because in His forbearance God had passed over the sins that were previously committed, to demonstrate at the present time His righteousness, that He might be just and the justifier of the one who has faith in Jesus."* Romans 3:24-26. The word *propitiation* in this text is the same Hebrew word as that of the mercy seat. Therefore, at the mercy seat in the Most Holy Place, which is the throne of God, *"Mercy triumphs over judgment."* James 2:13. This is possible only through what Jesus has done for us. With His death, *"Mercy and truth have met* together; *Righteousness and peace have kissed.*" Psalm 85:10.

Paul explained the symbolic significance of the entire sacrificial system of the Hebrew people in Hebrews 9:6-16. *"Now when these things had been thus prepared, the priests always went into the first part of the tabernacle, performing the services. But into the second part the high priest went alone once a year, not without blood, which he offered for himself and for the people's sins committed in ignorance; the Holy Spirit indicating this, that the way into the Holiest of All was not yet made manifest while the first tabernacle was still standing. It was symbolic for the present time in which both gifts and sacrifices are offered which cannot make him who performed the service perfect in regard to the conscience — concerned only with foods and drinks, various washings, and fleshly ordinances imposed until the time of reformation."*

"But Christ came as High Priest of the good things to come, with the greater and more perfect tabernacle not made with hands, that is, not of this creation. Not with the blood of goats and calves, but with His own blood He entered the Most Holy Place once for all, having obtained eternal redemption. For if the blood of bulls and goats and the ashes of a heifer, sprinkling the unclean, sanctifies for the purifying of the flesh, how much more shall the blood of Christ, who through the eternal Spirit offered Himself without spot to God, cleanse your conscience from dead works to serve the living God? And for this reason He is the Mediator of the new covenant, by means of death, for the redemption of the transgressions under the first covenant, that those who are called may receive the promise of the eternal inheritance."

Shekinah Glory
Although the Bible does not use the word 'Shekinah', it does

appear in many later Jewish writings. It simply means the presence of God on earth. It is used when referring to instances when God manifested Himself visibly, such as on Mount Sinai (see Exodus 24:9-18), in the Holy of Holies of the tabernacle (see Exodus 40:34-35), and in Solomon's Temple (see 1 Kings 8:10-11).

Shekinah is sometimes used to describe the great light that shone as evidence of God's presence in the Holy of Holies. How bright was this light? *"Now it was so, when Moses came down from Mount Sinai (and the two tablets of the Testimony were in Moses' hand when he came down from the mountain), that Moses did not know that the skin of his face shone while he talked with Him. So when Aaron and all the children of Israel saw Moses, behold, the skin of his face shone, and they were afraid to come near him"* Exodus 34:29-30. If the reflected glory of God was so bright that the people of Israel could not look at it, imagine what the brightness of the full glory of God is like. Peter, James and John also experienced this at Christ's transfiguration: *"And He was transfigured before them. His face shone like the sun, and His clothes became as white as the light . . . While he was still speaking, behold, a bright cloud overshadowed them; and suddenly a voice came out of the cloud, saying, ' This is My beloved Son, in whom I am well pleased. Hear Him!' And when the disciples heard it, they fell on their faces and were greatly afraid."* Matthew 17:2, 5-7. Paul saw Christ on the road to Damascus: *"Then last of all He was seen by me also, as by one born out of due time."* 1 Corinthians 15:8. Notice too, how Luke describes it, *"As he journeyed he came near Damascus, and suddenly a light shone around him from heaven. Then he fell to the ground, and heard a voice saying to him, 'Saul, Saul, why are you persecuting Me?' "* Acts 9:3-4.

The Glory of God

Due to his encounter with Christ on the road to Damascus, Paul was blind for three days until God healed him. God's presence was repeatedly manifested in the tabernacle by the glory that shone out of the Most Holy Place. (See Exodus 14:20 and 40:34-38; Leviticus 9:23-24; Numbers 14:10 and 16:19, 42). God's glory could be seen from within the holy place, the first apartment of the tabernacle. At times, it became so bright the priest had to leave the holy place, because it filled it completely. Just imagine how bright it will be when Christ returns. *"For whoever is ashamed of Me and My words, of him the Son of Man will be ashamed when He comes in His own glory, and in His Father's, and of the holy angels."* Luke 9:26. The combined brightness of the glory of the Father, of Christ, and of the holy angels will illuminate the entire earth. It is no wonder that *". . . the kings of the earth, the great men, the rich men, the commanders, the mighty men, every slave and every free man, hid themselves in the caves and in the rocks of the mountains, and said to the mountains and rocks, 'Fall on us and hide us from the face of Him who sits on the throne and from the wrath of the Lamb! For the great day of His wrath has come, and who is able to stand?'"* Revelation 6:15-17.

THE
SANCTUARY
PURE AND SIMPLE

CHAPTER 12

Israel's Annual Feast

Springtime Feasts

God instructed the children of Israel to keep seven annual feasts, which were divided into two groups: four in the spring, and three in the fall. Attendance at three of the seven annual feasts, Passover, Pentecost, and the Feast of Tabernacles, was compulsory for all men twenty years of age and above. They were to go up to Jerusalem, to the Sanctuary or Temple.

Passover

The springtime feasts started with the Passover, which was in commemoration of Israel's freedom from bondage in Egypt. It took place in the early spring, on the 14th day of the first month, just as the trees were budding and the flowers blooming, proclaiming the end of winter. Since travel was either by foot, or in a wagon drawn by a horse or donkey, groups traveling to Jerusalem had ample opportunity to visit with friends, and to enjoy the beauty of nature. The symbolism in the Passover service is full of meaning. The name Passover came from the instruction God gave Moses on the night of the 14th day of the first month. God instructed Israel that the angel of death would pass over the land, and that each family must be in its house. Each family was to sacrifice a Passover lamb, which represented Christ, and place its blood on the lentil and two doorposts of its house. In this way, when the destroying angel passed over and saw the blood, the first born of the family would not die (Exodus 12:12-13). *"And it came to pass at midnight that the Lord struck all the firstborn in the land of Egypt . . ."* (Exodus 12:29). How equally true this is today. No matter if one is rich or poor, free or in a prison cell, we must have the blood of Christ applied to our life to keep from dying the second death, that is, eternal death (Revelation 2:11). As Paul wrote in 1 Corinthians 5:7, *"For indeed Christ, our Passover, was sacrificed for us."* Consider the following comparisons between Christ and the Passover lamb:

- *"Again, the next day, John stood with two of his disciples. And looking at Jesus as He walked, he said, "Behold the Lamb of God!"* John 1:35-36.

- *". . . He was led as a sheep to the slaughter; And as a lamb before its shearer is silent, So He opened not His mouth."* Acts 8:32.

- *"but with the precious blood of Christ, as of a lamb without blemish and without spot."* 1 Peter 1:19-20.

Just as the Passover lamb was "without blemish" (Exodus 12:5), so Christ was without spot or blemish (1 Peter 1:19); and just as the Passover took place on the 14th day of the first month, Christ died at the time the Passover lamb was being offered. The instruction of Scripture was that not a bone of the Passover lamb was to be broken (Exodus 12:46). Even though the Roman soldiers broke the legs of the two thieves on either side of Jesus, they did not break Christ's legs; not one bone in His body was broken (John 19:36).

The Passover lamb was to be killed at twilight and eaten that night, leaving nothing for the next day (Exodus 12:6-10). If the family was small, they were to invite others to join them so that all of the lamb would be eaten that night. If any of it was left over, it was to be burned. Christ instituted the Lord's Supper on the evening before His crucifixion: *"And as they were eating, Jesus took bread, blessed and broke it, and gave it to the disciples and said, "Take, eat; this is My body"* Matthew 26:26.

Only Christ could fulfill these symbols. It would have been impossible for a man to arrange all these types and shadows of the Passover to meet their fulfillment in Him, since some of them he could not have arranged. This is yet another example of the strong evidence God has given mankind that Christ alone was the Lamb of God, the Savior of mankind. *"He indeed was foreordained before the foundation of the world, but was manifest in these last times for you . . ."* (1 Peter 1:19-21).

Feast of Unleavened Bread

The Feast of Unleavened Bread began on the 15th day of the seventh month, that is, on the day after the Passover: *"And on the fifteenth day of the same month is the Feast of Unleavened Bread to the Lord; seven days you must eat unleavened bread"* (Leviticus 23:6). This seven day feast began, and ended, with an annual Sabbath. Unlike the weekly Sabbaths which always occured on the seventh or last day of each week (Saturday), the annual Sabbaths occurred on the same dates each year, and could therefore fall on any day of the week. The Scripture tells us that leaven was a symbol of sin: *"Therefore let us keep the feast, not with old leaven, nor with the leaven of malice and wickedness, but with the unleavened bread of sincerity and truth"* 1 Corinthians 5:8. During the seven days of the feast, no leaven was to be eaten; they were to search their homes diligently to ensure all of it was gone. God is holy, and He wants His people to be holy. By the power of God, we can become *"a new creation,"* a new person, in Christ (2 Corinthians 5:17). Although all three members of the Godhead were involved in creation (Genesis 1:26), the most active agent was Jesus: *"All things were made through Him, and without Him nothing was made that was made"* (John 1:3). On the sixth day of creation week He finished His work of calling the world into existence, and pronounced it *"very good"* (Genesis 1:31). *"Then God blessed the seventh day and sanctified it, because in it He rested from all His work which God had created and made"* (Genesis 2:3). God blessed the seventh day of the week and sanctified it in commemoration of His great work of creation, the first of His two greatest works of love on mankind's behalf. God named the seventh day of the week, the Sabbath, which means rest, and God commanded mankind to rest on the seventh day of each week in honor of His perfect and finished work of creation.

This instruction is twice as applicable today, after the cross, when Sabbath rest also honors the second of God's two greatest works of love on mankind's behalf, our redemption, our spiritual re-creation, in Christ. It was not by accident that Christ died on the sixth day of the week, Friday, and then rested in the tomb over the seventh day of the week, the Sabbath. Just before breathing His last on the sixth day of the week, the same day God finished His great work of creation (Genesis 1:31), Jesus declared, *"It is finished!"* In other words, the earthly portion of mankind's redemption had been completed by God, in Christ. After living a sinless life by fulfilling all the demands of the law (Hebrews 4:15-16), *". . . Christ died for our sins"* at the exact time, and in the exact manner, the Scriptures prophesied that He would die (1 Corinthians 15:3). Jesus Christ is the only Person in history who wrote His autobiography, significant details, not only of His life, but also of His death, centuries before He was even born! Needless to say, that is something only He could have accomplished.

Upon perfectly completing the earthly portion of His work of our redemption, Jesus rested in the tomb over the Sabbath day, just as He rested following His great work of creation in Genesis 2:1-3. Jesus' closest followers also rested on the Sabbath, just as He had taught them to do: *"And the women who had come with Him from Galilee followed after, and they* observed the tomb and how His body was laid. Then they returned and prepared spices and fragrant oils. And they rested on the Sabbath according to the commandment" Luke 23:55-56. John 19:31 states that this Sabbath was a "high day," which meant that a weekly Sabbath and an annual Sabbath were falling on the same day. This is very significant because, as we shall see, it foretold how long Christ would be in the grave.

Offering of the First fruits

The offering of the firstfruits was part of the week constituting the Feast of Unleavened Bread. It took place on the sixteenth day of the month, the day after the annual Sabbath that began the Feast of Unleavened Bread. "And the Lord spoke to Moses, saying, "Speak to the children of Israel, and say to them: 'When you come into the land which I give to you, and reap its harvest, then you shall bring a sheaf of the firstfruits of your harvest to the priest. He shall wave the sheaf before the Lord, to be accepted on your behalf; on the day after the Sabbath the priest shall wave it" (Leviticus 23:9-11).

To review, according to the Scripture, the Passover took place on the 14th day of the first month. The feast of Unleavened Bread began the next day, the 15th, which was an annual Sabbath. Since John 19:31 states that the Sabbath following Jesus' crucifixion was a "high day," meaning it was both the weekly and an annual Sabbath, it had to have occurred on the 15th. As a result, the offering of the firstfruits occurred on the 16th, that is, "on the day after the Sabbath" (Levticus 23:11).

What did these three events have to do with how long Christ would remain in the grave? Paul gives us an indication in 1 Corinthians 15:4, "and that He was buried, and that He rose again the third day according to the Scriptures." Paul's statement "according to the Scriptures" cannot have referred to the New Testament, because it had not yet been written. In 1 Corinthians 5:7, Paul goes a step further in explaining the point he is making: *". . . For indeed Christ, our Passover, was sacrificed for us."* Paul continues in Chapter 15, verse 20: *"But now Christ is risen from the dead, and has become the first fruits of those who have fallen asleep."* There we have it. Since Christ is our Passover, He had to die on the 14th day of the seventh month, which He did. Christ completed the work of redemption on the 14th day, the Passover. He then rested in the tomb on the 15th day, the Sabbath. On the 16th day He then rose from the grave as the firstfruits.

All of these types or shadows meet their fulfillment in Christ. When the Pharisees came to Christ asking to see a sign, He answered them by saying, *". . . For as Jonah was three days and three nights in the belly of the great fish, so will the Son of Man be three days and three nights in the heart of the earth"* Matthew 12:38-40. Some people have difficulty with this text, but we need only consult the Bible to find when each day begins: *"God called the light Day, and the darkness He called Night. So the evening and the morning were the first day"* Genesis 1:5. In God's reckoning, the dark part of the day comes first. Time was measured this way until A.D. 1500 The following chart illustrates what was meant by three days and three nights:

Christ died around 3:00 p.m. on Friday, at the time the Passover lamb was being offered. He rested in the tomb during the Sabbath (Saturday,) and He arose Sunday morning while it was still dark. How then do we arrive at the "three days and three nights" of Matthew 12:40? In Christ's day, any part of a day was counted as one day. As two of Jesus' disciples told Him on the first day of the week (resurrection Sunday) as they walked along the road to Emmaus, *". . . Indeed, besides all this, today is the third day since these things happened."* (Luke 24:21). In commemoration of His death and resurrection, Christ gave us the ordinance of baptism: *"Therefore we were buried with Him through baptism into death, that just as Christ was raised from the dead by the glory of the Father, even so we also should walk in newness of life"* (Romans 6:4).

Pentecost

Pentecost was held fifty days after the waving of the first fruits. This feast was also called the Feast of Harvest, because it came at the end of the harvest, and was a feast of thanksgiving for the Lord's blessings. It was the last of the annual feasts in the first half of the year, which gave the grain time to ripen and mature, and it was one of the three feasts that was compulsory for the men to attend. They were to bring a liberal freewill offering according to how God had blessed them. It was a feast of great rejoicing in which everyone, the poor, the Levite, the afflicted and the stranger were invited to participate. Two rains were required in order to have a good harvest: one in the spring, called the former rain, and another at the end of the season, called the latter rain. The former rain gave the grain the moisture it needed to grow and develop, and the latter rain helped the grain to mature and ripen.

The prophet Joel applies this to the work of the Holy Spirit: *". . . And rejoice in the Lord your God; For He has given you the former rain faithfully, And He will cause the rain to come* down for you — *The former rain, and the latter rain in the first month. The threshing floors shall be full of wheat, and the vats shall overflow with new wine and oil."* (Joel 2:23-24). Christ went throughout Judea, sowing good seed by preaching *"the kingdom of God is at hand"* (Mark 1:15), healing the sick, and teaching the people the principles of the kingdom of heaven. At the end of three and a half years, only a 120 faithful stood on the Mount of Olives to watch Jesus ascend into heaven. That may not seem like much success after several years of hard work, but Pentecost was just ahead.

Fifty days later, the Holy Spirit was poured out as the former rain upon the waiting believers, setting them on fire. Filled with the Spirit of God, they went forth declaring the good news of the gospel: that the Son of God had risen from the grave, that He is the resurrection and the life, that God had secured mankind's salvation through Christ, and that man could have eternal life by believing in Christ. Under the power of the Holy Spirit, three thousand souls were converted in a single day by Peter's preaching (Acts 2:41). These conversions were not due to the work of the disciples, but were the direct result of Christ's ministry (Acts 2:32-36). The promise had been given, *"The threshing floors shall be full of wheat, and the vats shall overflow with new wine and oil."* (Joel 2:24). In ten short years, the gospel had gone to all of Asia Minor, and in 34 years it had covered the then-known world.

The latter rain, which is to help ripen the grain and prepare it for the harvest, is promised for the last days, that is, the time in which we live. This is a gift that is given only to Christians. How does one receive this gift of the Holy Spirit? During the Feast of Pentecost, Peter made a statement in answer to a question about the Holy Spirit: *"Then Peter said to them, "Repent, and let every one of you be baptized in the name of*

Jesus Christ for the remission of sins; and you shall receive the gift of the Holy Spirit" Acts 2:38.

Receiving the Holy Spirit involves four steps. The first step is repentance, in which a person acknowledges his sins, desires to stop sinning, and asks God to forgive him. The second step is baptism by immersion, which is how Scripture instructs us to be baptized: *"Or do you not know that as many of us as were baptized into Christ Jesus were baptized into His death? Therefore we were buried with Him through baptism into death, that just as Christ was raised from the dead by the glory of the Father, even so we also should walk in newness of life. For if we have been united together in the likeness of His death, certainly we also shall be in the likeness of His resurrection"* (Romans 6:3-5). Only baptism by immersion can properly represent death, burial, and resurrection, as the believer holds his breath, goes under the water, and then comes up out of the water a new person in Christ. All their prior sins washed away. The third step is surrendering one's will to Christ's control, walking as He walked. *"And we are His witnesses to these things, and so also is the Holy Spirit whom God has given to those who obey Him"* (Acts 5:32). The last step is to ask for the gift of the Holy Spirit: *"If you then, being evil, know how to give good gifts to your children, how much more will your heavenly Father give the Holy Spirit to those who ask Him!"* (Luke 11:13). Through these four steps, the Holy Spirit will be poured out in greater measure upon us, and prepare us for the second coming of Christ.

Autumn Feasts

Autumn has arrived. The crops have now been harvested and stored in barns. The heavy labor of plowing, preparing the soil for planting, tending the crops and finally harvesting them, is over. The people are now free to travel to Jerusalem to attend the feasts without worrying about things back home. The first Autumn feast came on the first day of the seventh month, which corresponded to our months of October and November.

The Feast of Trumpets

The lyrics of an old gospel song say, *"When the trumpet of the Lord shall sound and time shall be no more, and the morning breaks eternal bright and fair."* What a glorious day that will be. The book of Revelation speaks of seven angels, each one having a trumpet and announcing judgments that will fall upon the earth. When the seventh angel sounds its trumpet, the Kingdom of God is proclaimed (Revelation 11:15). The trumpet of God will be used to call the dead from the grave: *"For the Lord Himself will descend from heaven with a shout, with the voice of an archangel, and with the trumpet of God. And the dead in Christ will rise first."* (1 Thessalonians 4:16).

Trumpets figured prominently in the lives of the children of Israel. At Mt. Sinai, God instructed Moses to make two silver trumpets. They were to be used to assemble the people, to call them to prepare for war, and to alert them of when each tribe was to move out, as they traveled from one place to another. With the blowing of the trumpets, the walls of Jericho collapsed. The trumpets were to be blown at the beginning of each month, when the people offered a burnt offering or a peace offering, and when they celebrated a day of gladness. At the dedication of the temple in the days of Solomon, the priests were so skilled that 120 priests blowing trumpets could make them sound as one trumpet (2 Chronicles 5:12,13).

The trumpet was used frequently, because it served as a

memorial. It reminded the people that the Lord was their God (Numbers 10:10), that they were to place their trust in Him, and worship and obey only Him. They were entering into the land of the Philistines, in which all the different nations worshiped pagan gods. The trumpets were a daily reminder that the Lord their God was their Protector, who had brought them out of bondage in Egypt, and had given them the land of Canaan. He alone was to be worshiped. One special day each year, the first day of the seventh month, was reserved for the blowing of the trumpets (Numbers 29:1). That day was a holy assembly during which no work was to be done; it was to be given completely to the Lord. It served as a warning, for in just ten days the solemn Day of Atonement would begin.

Day of Atonement

The Day of Atonement took place on the 10th day of the seventh month. It was considered the most sacred of all the feasts. If a man or woman did not participate in the Day of Atonement, they were cut off from the children of Israel. The day was a holy assembly known as an annual Sabbath, so that no work was to be done on that day. The people were to gather at the Sanctuary or Temple, examine their lives, and confess all their un-confessed sins. The Day of Atonement was a cleansing of the Sanctuary. It was not a physical cleansing, but rather a symbolic cleansing of all the sins that had been brought to the Sanctuary during the preceding year. When an individual brought a sacrifice of a lamb or goat to the Sanctuary and placed their hands upon the head of the sacrifice, confessing their sins, their sins were vicariously passed from them to the animal. The animal was then slain by the repentant sinner, and blood of the sacrifice was taken by the priest into the holy place of the Sanctuary, where some of it was placed on the horns of the altar of incense, and sprinkled on the veil. In this way, the sins were transferred from the repentant sinner to the sacrificial animal, and then from the blood of the lamb or goat to the Sanctuary. This went on day-in and day-out for the entire year, during which the Sanctuary symbolically collected the sins of the people.

Once each year, on the Day of Atonement, the Sanctuary was symbolically cleansed. The High Priest would select two young goats and cast lots for them; one lot fell on the Lord's goat and the other lot on the scapegoat. The high priest would not place his hands on the head of the Lord's goat and confess the sins of Israel, because this service was for cleansing, not for the forgiveness of sins. In type, all the accumulated sins in the Sanctuary were passed from the High Priest to the Lord's goat, and the Lord's goat was then slain as a sin offering for the people. The blood of the Lord's goat was then taken by the high priest to the second compartment of the Sanctuary, the Most Holy Place. This was the only time the High Priest was allowed into this room each year, for he was entering into the very presence of God.

The morning of the Day of Atonement, the High Priest had offered a bull for the sins of himself and his family, for he could not appear before God with his sins un-confessed and remain alive. A cloud of incense from the censer he carried covered him as he stood before the mercy seat, above which were the two golden cherubim, and the Shekinah glory of God. Dipping his finger into the blood of the Lord's goat, the High Priest sprinkled it seven times on the mercy seat, cleansing the Most Holy Place of the sins that had accumulated in the Sanctuary during the past year. When he left the Most Holy Place, he stopped in the Holy Place and sprinkled the blood of the Lord's goat on the altar of incense, cleansing it of all the sins. He then exited the Sanctuary into the court and cleansed the altar of sacrifice by sprinkling some of the blood upon it. In this way, atonement was made for the Sanctuary.

The High Priest now placed his hands on the head of the live goat, known as the scapegoat, and confessed the sins, transgressions, and iniquities of the children of Israel. In type, this transferred all the sins to the scapegoat, which represents the devil. Satan, the originator of sin, must bear the responsibility for it. (See Ezekiel 28:11-19). The scapegoat was then led into an uninhabited area by a suitable man, and abandoned to die in the wilderness. The bodies of the sacrifices were carried outside the camp of Israel, and burned to ashes. The Sanctuary was now cleansed, since all trace of sin had been removed.

This entire service is so full of symbolism that I will not explain it here, but in the next two chapters we will see how perfectly God illustrated the great plan of redemption.

Feast of Tabernacles

This was the last of the seven annual feasts. It began on the 15th day of the seventh month, which was also the end of the Jewish sacred year and lasted seven days. Whereas, the Day of Atonement was a time for each person to solemnly search their lives to ensure they were right with God. Just five days later, was a feast of rejoicing that the crops were harvested and safely stored in the barns. Looking over the past year, they were to dwell on God's blessings and, with gladness in their hearts, journey to the city of Jerusalem to keep the Feast of Tabernacles. It was called the Feast of Tabernacles because they were to build, and live in, booths of palm branches, willow trees, or the boughs of thick trees. These were built on any vacant lot, and even on top of the houses. This feast was to remind them of the 40 years their forefathers spent living in tents in the wilderness, following their deliverance from Egypt. This was one of the three annual feasts that every male aged 20 and above was required to attend.

On the last day of this feast, the people would all gather in the courtyard of the temple, and a couple priests would carry two large flagons. Following the priests, the people would march around the courtyard, singing songs and quoting Scripture. Making their way through the gates of the temple and down the streets of Jerusalem, they praised God for His goodness to them. Exiting the city gate, they proceeded down the hill to a brook called Kedron. The priests would dip the two flagons into the brook, filling them with water; then the priests and the people would make their way back to the courtyard. Here, one of the priests would take one of the jugs of water, while the other priest would take a jug of wine. The priests would pour the two jugs simultaneously into a basin, mingling the water and wine together before it flowed through a pipe back to the brook Kedron. This service served to remind the people how God had so mercifully supplied them with water for 40 years in the desert.

In Jesus' day, just as the priests were pouring the water and wine into the basin, Jesus called out saying, ". . . *If anyone thirsts, let him come to Me and drink. He who believes in Me, as the Scripture has said, out of his heart will flow rivers of living water.*" (John 7:37-38). Christ is the One who was with Israel during its 40 years in the wilderness of Sinai, supplying all their needs, including food, water, clothing and protection: "*all ate the same spiritual food, and all drank the same spiritual drink. For they drank of that spiritual Rock that followed them, and that Rock was Christ.*" (1 Corinthians 10:3, 4). We no longer keep this feast, because there was always an offering connected with the feast. The sacrifice of animals came to an end when the true Lamb of God died on the cross of Calvary *"But this Man, after He had offered one sacrifice for sins forever, sat down at the right hand of God"* Hebrews 10:12. When the veil of the temple was torn in two from top to bottom, opening the way into the Most Holy Place, it signified that the Sanctuary service here on earth had come to an end. All of the feasts we have studied pointed forward to Christ and had their fulfillment in Him, which is why we no longer keep them today.

However, studying the feasts teaches us many wonderful lessons about salvation, judgment, last day events, the new earth, and heaven, so it is well-worth our time to study them. It helps us to understand more clearly what a wonderful God and Savior we have.

THE
SANCTUARY
PURE AND SIMPLE

CHAPTER 13

Christ Our High Priest

Christic the High Priest

"Therefore, in all things He had to be made like His brethren, that He might be a merciful and faithful High Priest in things pertaining to God, to make propitiation for the sins of the people. For in that He Himself has suffered, being tempted, He is able to aid those who are tempted" (Hebrews 2:17-18). A merciful and faithful High Priest must, on one hand, be able to understand man; yet on the other hand he must be able to understand the love and justice of God. The only One who could do this was Jesus Christ. He became man and was tempted and tried as we are, yet He was without sin. *"For we do not have a High Priest who cannot sympathize with our weaknesses, but was in all points tempted as we are, yet without sin. Let us therefore come boldly to the throne of grace, that we may obtain mercy and find grace to help in time of need"* (Hebrews 4:15-16). As a result, Jesus is qualified to represent mankind before His Father, for He is able to sympathize with our weaknesses and failures. However, it is also necessary that humanity's Redeemer be able to understand the problem of sin from God's viewpoint, and that requires someone with a divine nature. Jesus perfectly understands God's side, since He is one with the Father. (See John 10:30). He can minister to both sides, since He was entirely human, and completely divine.

Jesus Christ, the Lamb of God, served as our Savior on earth. He gave His life for the salvation of all humanity. At His ascension, Jesus returned to heaven to serve as our High Priest. *"Now this is the main point of the things we are saying: We have such a High Priest, who is seated at the right hand of the throne of the Majesty in the heavens, a Minister of the sanctuary and of the true tabernacle which the Lord erected, and not man"* (Hebrews 8:1-2).

Christic the Mediator

"But now He has obtained a more excellent ministry, inasmuch as He is also Mediator of a better covenant, which was established on better promises" (Hebrews 8:6). The Scripture is very clear on what was wrong with the old covenant. *"For if that first covenant had been faultless, then no place would have been sought for a second. Because finding fault with them, He says: "Behold, the days are coming, says the Lord, when I will make a new covenant with the house of Israel and with the house of Judah"* (Hebrews 8:7-8). When Moses explained God's first covenant to Israel, they replied, *"All that the LORD has spoken we will do"* (Exodus 19:8). However, they did not live up to the agreement and constantly refused to comply with the covenant. As a result, the covenant needed to be made with someone who could keep it. By taking on the nature of man, Christ could be the Mediator of a better covenant, since the covenant would be established on His word, and not man's. All believers have His promise; *"For this is the covenant that I will make with the house of Israel after those days, says the LORD: I will put My laws in their mind and write them on their hearts; and I will be their God, and they shall be My people."* (Hebrews 8:10).

The levitical priesthood was limited in its effectiveness and consistency, because the high priest could only mediate as long as he lived. At his death, the mediatorial relationship changed based on the values of the new high priest. (See 1 Samuel 2:12-17). Blessedly, this is not the case with Jesus Christ: *"But He, because He continues forever, has an unchangeable priesthood. Therefore He is also able to save to the uttermost those who come to God through Him, since He always lives to make intercession for them."* Hebrews 7:24-25.

The responsibility of changing heart and mind is God's: (See Jeremiah 13:23 and Psalm 51:10). Having the willingness to be changed is our duty, *"being confident of this very thing, that He who has begun a good work in you will complete it until the day of Jesus Christ"* (Philippians 1:6).

Order of Melchizedek

The Melchizedek order of the priesthood existed long before the Levitical priesthood, and was superior to it. Who was Melchizedek? *"Then Melchizedek king of Salem brought out bread and wine; he was the priest of God Most High"* (Genesis 14:18). Note that the Scripture states *"the priest"* and not, *"a priest,"* indicating that he was the only one. Scripture uses very few words in describing Melchizedek. However, those words speak volumes. (See Genesis 14:18-20, and Hebrews 5:5-10 and 7:1-28). Why was the priesthood of Melchizedek superior to the Levitical priesthood? Paul tells us that Jesus was *"called by God as High Priest 'according to the order of Melchizedek.' "* (Hebrews 5:10).

Abraham lived before there was a Levitical priesthood. Therefore, Melchizedek, *"the priest of God Most High"* (Genesis 14:18), received Abraham's tithe. Since both Christ and Melchizedek existed before Abraham (John 8:58, Hebrews 7:1-3), Paul ties Christ to the order of Melchizedek. *"And it is yet far more evident if, in the likeness of Melchizedek, there arises another priest who has come, not according to the law of a fleshly commandment, but according to the power of an endless life. For He testifies: 'You are a priest forever according to the order of Melchizedek' "* (Hebrews 7:15-17). This Scripture is fulfilled, in that Christ is both our High Priest and Mediator. He is uniquely qualified to represent both God and man. At the same time, He is the *". . . King of kings and Lord of lords."*

(1 Timothy 6:15). Jesus Christ is the only person who ever existed with the credentials to fulfill both offices. He will soon return to set up His everlasting kingdom.

The responsibility for the tabernacle rested on the tribe of Levi, because they were loyal to God when the golden calf was worshiped at the base of Mt. Sinai. (See Exodus 32:25-29). Among their responsibilities was caring for the Sanctuary by maintaining it, and transporting it from place to place during Israel's travels. Both Moses and Aaron were of the tribe of Levi. Because of Aaron's service to God, the priesthood was bestowed on him and his descendants. The rest of the Levites were to assist them in their work.

For centuries, all high priests were descendants of Levi. That changed in the days of Eli, whose sons became so corrupt that Samuel, who was of the tribe of Ephraim, became the high priest (See 1 Samuel 2:27-36). In other words, there were times when someone served as high priest who was not of the tribe of Levi. Jesus was of the tribe of Judah, not Levi, and was a priest, *"According to the order of Melchizedek."* (Hebrews 7:17). (See Hebrews 7:11-18).

Israel's king usually came from the tribe of Judah, and it was foretold that Jesus would be a king (Matthew 2:2). Pilate asked Jesus, *"'Are You the King of the Jews?' He answered him and said, 'It is as you say'"* (Luke 23:3). Jesus fulfilled both positions of King and High Priest.

Christ Our Forerunner

Hebrews 6:20 states, *"where the forerunner has entered for us, even Jesus, having become High Priest forever according to the order of Melchizedek."* A *"forerunner"* is simply someone who goes before, or ahead of. Jesus Christ went ahead of us so we can know that, just as He was victorious over sin and death, we too, can be victorious through faith in Him. *"Seeing then that we have a great High Priest who has passed through the heavens, Jesus the Son of God, let us hold fast our confession. For we do not have a High Priest who cannot sympathize with our weaknesses, but was in all points tempted as we are, yet without sin. Let us therefore come boldly to the throne of grace, that we may obtain mercy and find grace to help in time of need"* (Hebrews 4:14-16). Jesus walked through this sinful world just as we must do. He had to face every temptation in His humanity, without divine help other than faith in His Father. As the Forerunner, He showed that complete victory over sin is possible, and that we can have complete victory also by trusting in Him.

As the great Forerunner, Jesus was victorious over death and the grave. *"Yea, though I walk through the valley of the shadow of death, I will fear no evil; for You are with me"* (Psalm 23:4). To the believer, death is but a sleep, from which one will awaken to everlasting life. Jesus' resurrection from the grave gives every follower of Christ hope of eternal life. Just as He, the *"Resurrection and the Life"* (John 11:25), went before us and rose from the grave, the redeemed dead will also rise to new life.

Jesus preceded us to heaven and promised: *"Let not your heart be troubled; you believe in God, believe also in Me. In my Father's house are many mansions; if it were not so, I would have told you. I go to prepare a place for you. And if I go and prepare a place for you, I will come again and receive you to Myself; that where I am, there you may be also."* (John 14:1-3). Thank God for the Forerunner Jesus Christ! Let us give Him all honor, glory, and praise, for He made our salvation sure.

Sin Bearer

Of all the titles given to Christ, "Sin Bearer" carries the most meaning, for it expresses Christ's selfless love for you, for me, and for all mankind. As we have previously studied, on the annual Day of Atonement, the High Priest symbolically bore the sins of the children of Israel that had accumulated in the Sanctuary during the past year until they were cleansed by the blood of the Lord's goat, and then placed on the head of the scapegoat, which was banished into the wilderness forever. In the same way, Christ is bearing the sins of the world until they are cleansed at the end of time by the blood of the *"Lamb of God"*. *"For Christ has not entered the holy places made with hands, which are copies of the true, but into heaven itself, now to appear in the presence of God for us; not that He should offer Himself often, as the high priest enters the Most Holy Place every year with blood of another — He then would have had to suffer often since the foundation of the world; but now, once at the end of the ages, He has appeared to put away sin by the sacrifice of Himself. And as it is appointed for men to die once, but after this the judgment, so Christ was offered once to bear the sins of many. To those who eagerly wait for Him He will appear a second time, apart from sin, for salvation"* (Hebrews 9:24-28).

O matchless love! God's free gift of salvation, by grace and through faith in Jesus Christ, is the greatest gift that has ever been offered to mankind. It is a gift beyond all human understanding. We occasionally learn of a person who was willing to give his or her life to save other people. Jesus stated that *nobody has "greater love"* (John 15:13-14), yet Christ's love surpassed that. His death was not one person dying for another person, it was God dying for all humanity. Jesus' sacrificial death was the Creator dying for those He created. Paul explains it this way: *"For He made Him who knew no sin to be sin for us, that we might become the righteousness of God in Him*" (2 Corinthians 5:21). It is impossible to imagine a more priceless, more precious gift! If you are but willing to receive it, through faith in Him, Christ the Sin Bearer wants to take your sins, and all the resulting guilt, condemnation and shame, and give you His righteousness in return. If you are willing, His perfect righteousness is available to you, just for the asking.

He longs for you to ask Him for it. Why not pause and do so, just now?

THE
SANCTUARY
PURE AND SIMPLE

CHAPTER 14

Incredible Prophecy

Cleansing of the Sanctuary

Prophecy is unique to the Bible. There are no prophecies in the Koran, in the writings of Buddha, in the book of Mormon, etc. Prophecy accomplishes several purposes. It places God's stamp of authenticity on the Scriptures. It gives us guidance for the future. It also helps us to know where to place our trust. In Isaiah 1:18, God gives us this wonderful invitation: *"Come now, and let us reason together."* God is confident in extending this invitation to us, because He knows the truths He shares with us in His Holy Scriptures appeal to the common sense, the "reason," He created us with. In Psalm 18:30, God gives us this wonderful promise: *". . . The word of the LORD is proven."* You see, faith in the Bible and in its Author, Jesus Christ (See John 1:1-4,14 and 16:13-14), is not based upon thin air, it is based upon substantive evidence: *"Now faith is the substance of things hoped for, the evidence of things not seen"* (Hebrews 11:1).

There are over 2000 prophecies in the Bible. However, we will concentrate here on just one of them. Only by first understanding the Sanctuary can we then understand this incredible prophecy. It identifies the year of Christ's death 500 years before He was even born. It *proves* that Jesus was the promised Messiah of the Old Testament, and it shows where we are in the stream of time. The Day of Atonement was dedicated to the cleansing of the earthly sanctuary: *"For on that day the priest shall make atonement for you, to cleanse you, that you may be clean from all your sins before the Lord"* Leviticus 16:30. This prophecy also explains the specific time God has appointed for the cleansing of the heavenly sanctuary. *". . . God shall judge the righteous and the wicked, for there is a time there for every purpose and for every work"* (Ecclesiastes 3:17).

The Vision Given Daniel

"*. . . For two thousand three hundred days; then the sanctuary shall be cleansed*" (Daniel 8:14). Clearly, this prophecy involves the Sanctuary. The term "*cleansing of the sanctuary*" is synonymous with "*Day of Atonement*" or "*Day of Judgment.*" At the end of Chapter 8, Daniel admits to being baffled by the vision: "*And I, Daniel, fainted and was sick for days; afterward I arose and went about the king's business. I was astonished by the vision, but no one understood it*" (Daniel 8:27).

The Vision Explained

Three years elapsed from the time Daniel "fainted and was sick for days" (Daniel 8:27). The ninth chapter begins with Daniel praying for understanding. "*In the first year of Darius the son of Ahasuerus . . . I set my face toward the Lord God to make request by prayer and supplications, with fasting, sackcloth, and ashes*" (Daniel 9:1-3). When we pray, we must be persevering and patient. God always answers prayer, but He does so according to His time schedule, not ours.

Daniel gained some understanding from a contemporary prophet, Jeremiah: "*I, Daniel, understood by the books the number of the years specified by the word of the Lord through Jeremiah the prophet, that He would accomplish seventy years in the desolations of Jerusalem*" (Daniel 9:2). After Daniel's fervent supplication for help, God sent the angel Gabriel to explain the vision: "*Yes, while I was speaking in prayer, the man Gabriel, whom I had seen in the vision at the beginning, being caused to fly swiftly, reached me about the time of the evening offering. And he informed me, and talked with me, and said, 'O Daniel, I have now come forth to give you skill to understand. At the beginning of your supplications the command went out, and I have come to tell you, for you are greatly beloved; therefore consider the matter, and understand the vision' "* (Daniel 9:21-23).

70 Weeks

As Gabriel is explaining this vision, bear in mind that it was the *2300 days* of Daniel 8:13-14, which Daniel did not understand. Daniel 9:24 states, *"Seventy weeks are determined for your people* [Daniel's people, the Jews] *and for your holy city, to finish the transgression, to make an end of sins, to make reconciliation for iniquity, to bring in everlasting righteousness, to seal up vision and prophecy, and to anoint the Most Holy."* Since the *"seventy weeks"* is only one part of the 2300 day prophecy cannot be separated from that time period, for to do so would give us an incomplete picture. God has given a rule to help us understand time prophecies. The rule is that one *prophetic* day in time prophecy represents one *literal* year. *". . . I have laid on you a day for each year."* Ezekiel 4:6. *". . . for each day you shall bear your guilt one year"* Numbers 14:34.

The most convincing fact is that the time prophecies have been precisely fulfilled based upon this principle. You will find this to be true with the prophecies of Daniel, Chapters 7 and 9, as well as, Revelation, Chapters 11, 12, and 13. We know this principal of interpreting time prophecy is correct because, very simply, it works! Follow carefully how perfectly it unveils the events that are to take place.

Applying the "day for a year" principal, the *"two thousand three hundred days"* of Daniel 8:14 refer to 2300 literal years. It is the longest time prophecy in the Bible. In Daniel 9:24, the angel Gabriel begins to divide the 2300 years into segments by explaining the first *"seventy weeks"*. When we multiply 70 weeks times 7 days per week, we calculate 490 days/years. Gabriel now explains to Daniel what will happen during the first 490 years of the 2300-year period.

69 Weeks

"Know therefore and understand, That from the going forth of the command to restore and build Jerusalem until Messiah the Prince, there shall be seven weeks and sixty-two weeks; the street shall be built again, and the wall, Even in troublesome times." Daniel 9:25. This 69 weeks or 483 days/years (7 + 62 = 69 X 7 = 483) is the first part of the seventy weeks/490 years, which is itself the first part of the 2300 years.

Daniel 9:25 is very significant, because it gives us the starting point for the 2300 day/year prophecy of Daniel 8:14. *". . . From the going forth of the command to restore and build Jerusalem . . ."* The command or decree to restore and build Jerusalem was given by King Artaxerxes of the Medo-Persian Empire in the fall of 457 B.C. (See Ezra 7:11-26). Therefore, beginning with the fall of 457 B.C. and proceeding forward 483 years, we arrive at the fall of A.D. 27 (remember, when going from B.C. to A.D. always add one year, because there was no year zero).

What happened in A.D. 27? The angel Gabriel told Daniel it would be 69 weeks *"until Messiah the Prince"*. The gospel of Luke confirms Jesus' fulfillment of this: *"Now in the fifteenth year of the reign of Tiberius Caesar . . ."* Luke 3:1. Secular history records that the fifteenth year of Tiberius Caesar's reign was indeed A.D. 27. Luke continues, *"When all the people were baptized, it came to pass that Jesus also was baptized; and while He prayed, the heaven was opened. And the Holy Spirit descended in bodily form like a dove upon Him, and a voice came from heaven which said, 'You are My beloved Son; in You I am well pleased.' Now Jesus Himself began His ministry at about thirty years of age . . ."* (Luke 3:21-23). Christ alone perfectly fits the time window predicted in this prophecy. Jesus Christ began His ministry as the Messiah *precisely* on time, according to God's own prophetic clock!

70th Week

We have looked at 483 years (69 weeks) of the 490 years (70 weeks) determined upon Daniel's people, the Jews; which leaves 7 years (1 week) of the 70 years remaining. Many Bible students refer to this week as the *70th week*. Daniel explains, *"Then He shall confirm a covenant with many for one week; But in the middle of the week He shall brings an end to sacrifice and offering"* (Daniel 9:27). The 69 weeks brought us to the fall of A.D. 27, and Daniel 9:27 foretold that Messiah would *"bring an end to sacrifice and offering"* in the middle of the 70th week. Half of 7 years is 3½ years (the middle of the 70th week), and adding 3½ years to the fall of A.D. 27, brings us to the spring of A.D. 31, which is when Jesus was crucified!

Christ's ministry lasted 3½ years, from the fall of A.D. 27 to the spring of A.D. 31. He was crucified in the spring of A.D. 31, in the middle of the 70th prophetic week, exactly as this prophecy foretold He would be. It accurately foretold the death of Jesus Christ over 500 years before He was even born! *"And when they had come to the place called Calvary, there they crucified Him, and the criminals, one on the right hand and the other on the left"* (Luke 23:33). When Jesus died, *"Then, behold, the veil of the temple was torn in two from top to bottom; and the earth quaked, and the rocks were split."* Matthew 27:51. The miraculous rending of the temple's veil, which separated the Holy Place from the Most Holy Place, showed that the sacrifices and offerings had ended. The *true* Lamb of God had given His life for the sins of the world. The *proof* God has given us for His word (Psalm 18:30), the *substantive evidence*

He has lovingly given us upon which to build our faith in Him (Hebrews 11:1), is incontrovertible!

According to the prophecy, *"Seventy weeks are determined for your people"* (Daniel 9:24), that is, the Jews. Three and a half years of the 70th week remain. Adding 3½ years to the spring of A.D. 31 brings us to the fall of A.D. 34, which is when the Jewish leaders, in an act of defiance, stoned the first Christian martyr, Stephen, to death. (See Acts, chapters 6 and 7). This event occurred exactly 490 years after Artaxerxes' decree for the Jewish people to return to Jerusalem.

The stoning of Stephen marked the end of the seventy week/490 year probationary period God had given the Jewish people, *"To finish the transgression, to make an end of sins, to make reconciliation for iniquity, to bring in everlasting righteousness, to seal up vision and prophecy, and to anoint the Most Holy"* (Daniel 9:24).

Since the Jewish people had not returned to God by accepting Christ, and by taking the gospel to the Gentiles, Jesus' disciples were impressed to immediately begin taking the gospel to the Gentiles. The Scripture is clear that the Jewish people were to have been a light to the Gentiles, but they had failed in their responsibility. *"Then Paul and Barnabas grew bold and said, "It was necessary that the word of God should be spoken to you first; but since you reject it, and judge yourselves unworthy of everlasting life, behold, we turn to the Gentiles. For so the Lord has commanded us: 'I have set you as a light to the Gentiles, That you should be for salvation to the ends of the earth'"* (Acts 13:46-47). Just as the prophecy foretold, in the fall of A.D. 34, Saul of Tarsus was converted on the road to Damascus. (See Acts 9:1-22). Saul became Paul, the Apostle to the Gentiles.

At the same time, God also showed Peter that the Gospel was

to be taken to the Gentiles: *"Then he said to them, 'You know how unlawful it is for a Jewish man to keep company with or go to one of another nation. But God has shown me that I should not call any man common or unclean' "* Acts 10:28. Precisely as prophesied, the gospel went to the Gentiles at the end of the 490 years. The Sanctuary service on earth had come to an end, for the true Lamb of God to which it pointed, had given His life for the world. This opened the door for the gospel to go to all humanity.

Day of Judgment

Looking at the first 70 weeks, or 490 prophetic years, of the 2300 day/year prophecy. It has placed us in the fall of A.D. 34, 2300 minus 490 equals 1810 years of the prophecy remaining. Adding 1810 years to the fall of A.D. 34 brings us to the fall of A.D. 1844, which is when the cleansing of the Sanctuary, that is, the day of judgment, would begin in heaven. We know this because this prophecy cannot be referring to the Sanctuary or temple on earth, for it was destroyed during the destruction of Jerusalem in A.D. 70 Therefore, the prophecy has to refer to the *true* temple in heaven, upon which the earthly Sanctuary was patterned. *"After these things I looked, and behold, the temple of the tabernacle of the testimony in heaven was opened"* (Revelation 15:5).

Daniel describes the beginning of the judgment when Jesus, our High Priest, appears before His Father to intercede for us: *"I was watching in the night visions, And behold, One like the Son of Man, coming with the clouds of heaven! He came to the Ancient of Days, and they brought Him near before Him . . . and a judgment was made in favor of the saints of the Most High, and the time came for the saints to possess the kingdom"* (Daniel 7:13, 22). The high priest appeared before God once each year for the cleansing of the Sanctuary on earth. Christ, our true High Priest, is appearing before His Father only once for the cleansing of the Sanctuary in heaven (See Hebrews 9:23-28). Christ began the cleansing of the heavenly Sanctuary, and the judgment of the living, in A.D. 1844 He is now at work in Heaven examining our records in the Book of Life, Revelation 3:5, the Book of Remembrance, Malachi 3:16, and the Book of Iniquity, Jeremiah 2:22.

All the sins of the saints are being transferred from the heavenly temple to the true Lord's goat/the Sin-Bearer, Jesus Christ. His blood makes atonement for them. Following Jesus' second coming, those sins will be placed on Satan, the *real* scapegoat. He will be bound to the wilderness of this desolate earth for a thousand years, and will deceive the nations no more until the thousand years are finished. (See Revelation 20:1-3). The redeemed of all ages will have returned to heaven with Jesus. (See 1 Thessalonians 4:13-18), and all the living wicked will have been slain by the brightness of Jesus' second coming. (See Revelation 6:12-17 and Jeremiah 4:23-27).

Now, for one thousand years, Satan must bear the guilt and regret for the sin, degradation and death he caused. During the thousand years, the Judgment of the wicked will take place (See Revelation 20:4), and the saints will participate in the Judgment (1 Corinthians 6:3). God intends to leave no question in the minds of anyone that He has been perfectly loving, just, and fair regarding how He has dealt with each of the condemned. The redeemed will examine every case before the wicked receive their punishment of the *second* death, that is, *eternal* death (Revelation 21:8). God's love, justice, and fairness will be evident to all before He forever eradicates sinners and sin from the universe (Nahum 1:9).

At the end of the thousand years, in the resurrection of condemnation, God will resurrect all the wicked who have ever lived. (See John 5:28-29). Satan and all the wicked will stand before the Great White Throne Judgment. (See Revelation 20:11-13). Satan orchestrated the fall of humanity, therefore, he is implicated in the sins of all the wicked. As a result, he must also stand before the Great White Throne Judgment, as will all of his angel-turned-demon followers. Satan, his demons, and all of condemned humanity will acknowledge that God has been perfectly righteous and just in how He has dealt with sin and rebellion. (See Romans 14:10-11). Since they rejected God's free gift of Christ's atoning death for them, every condemned human being will acknowledge that he or she must die the second, eternal death for their own sins. (See Ezekiel 18:30-32 and Proverbs 8:36). Fire will then come down from God out of heaven and devour this sin-polluted planet, along with Satan, his evil angels, and all the wicked upon it. (See Revelation 20:7-9, and 2 Peter 3:10-12). Sinners and sin will be no more, forever (Nahum 1:9).

God will then create new heavens and a new earth to be His eternal home with the redeemed, and the kingdom of God will reign throughout eternity. (See Psalm 37:10-11, 2 Peter 3:13, and Revelation 21:1-5).

"He who testifies to these things says, 'Surely I am coming quickly.' Amen. Even so, come, Lord Jesus!

The grace of our Lord Jesus Christ be with you all. Amen." Revelation 22:20-21.

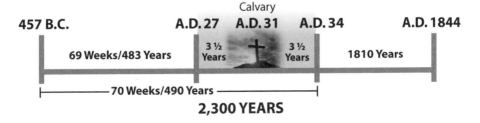

THE
SANCTUARY
PURE AND SIMPLE

CHAPTER 15

The New Jerusalem

The New Jerusalem

According to the Scriptures, there is no temple in the New Jerusalem: *"But I saw no temple in it, for the Lord God Almighty and the Lamb are its temple"* (Revelation 21:22). The veil in the earthly temple, which separated the Holy Place from the Most Holy Place, was removed by the death of Christ. Due to His mediation on mankind's behalf, no longer does anything stand between sinful man and a holy God. We can now enter directly into the throne room of God, into His very presence. We can *". . . come boldly to the throne of grace, that we may obtain mercy and find grace to help in time of need"* (Hebrews 4:16 and 1 John 1:9).

"And I heard a loud voice from heaven saying, 'Behold, the tabernacle of God is with men, and He will dwell with them, and they shall be His people, and God Himself will be with them and be their God.'" Revelation 21:3. God and the Lamb are in the New Jerusalem, and nothing more needs to be added. *"And the city had no need of the sun or of the moon to shine in it, for the glory of God illuminated it, and the Lamb is its light . . . But there shall by no means enter it anything that defiles, or causes an abomination or a lie, but only those who are written in the Lamb's Book of Life"* Revelation 21:23, 27.

The New Jerusalem will contain the tree of life: *"And he showed me a pure river of water of life, clear as crystal, proceeding from the throne of God and of the Lamb. In the middle of its street, and on either side of the river, was the tree of life, which bore twelve fruits, each tree yielding its fruit every month. The leaves of the tree were for the healing of the nations. And there shall be no more curse, but the throne of God and of the Lamb shall be in it, and His servants shall serve Him. They shall see His face, and His name shall be on their foreheads. There shall be no night there: They need no lamp nor light of the sun, for the Lord*

God gives them light. And they shall reign forever and ever" Revelation 22:1-5. Mankind lost access to the tree of life, as well as the conditional immortality God had created us with, at the fall. *"Then the LORD God said, 'Behold, the man has become like one of Us, to know good and evil. And now, lest he put out his hand and take also of the tree of life, and eat, and live forever'—therefore the LORD God sent him out of the garden of Eden to till the ground from which he was taken. So He drove out the man; and He placed cherubim at the east of the garden of Eden, and a flaming sword which turned every way, to guard the way to the tree of life"* (Genesis 3:22-24). Thanks to the saving work of the Lamb of God, mankind will once again have access to the tree of life in the new earth: *" 'For as the new heavens and the new earth which I will make shall remain before Me,' says the LORD, 'so shall your descendants and your name remain. And it shall come to pass that from one New Moon to another, and from one Sabbath to another, all flesh shall come to worship before Me,' says the LORD"* (Isaiah 66:22-23).

From the description given in the Scriptures, the New Jerusalem is a temple, and the saved will go there to worship. As we have previously covered, the second part of the earthly Sanctuary and Temple was called the Most Holy Place, where the presence of God dwelt. This was considered God's throne, because He spoke to the children of Israel from above the mercy seat that was located between the two cherubim. In each case, the Most Holy place was shaped like a cube, meaning that its length, width, and height were equal. In Revelation 21:16, John describes the New Jerusalem as follows: *"The city is laid out as a square, its length is as great as its breadth. And he measured the city with a reed: twelve thousand furlongs. Its length, breath, and height are equal."* Since there are eight furlongs in a mile, the New Jerusalem is fifteen hundred miles in length, width, and height, which is approximately the size of the state of Colorado.

The Bible continues to expand our understanding by telling us, *"Then I was given a reed like a measuring rod. And the angel stood, saying, 'Rise and measure the temple of God, the altar, and those who worship there. But leave out the court which is outside the temple, and do not measure it, for it has been given to the Gentiles.' "* (Revelation 11:1-2). The court represents the earth, where the Lamb of God was sacrificed for us. It is not needed in the New Jerusalem because the debt for our sins has already been paid, by God, in Christ. Behold, old things have passed away. All things have been made new.

Let us now consider what the Scripture states about the throne of God, where the saved will worship Him. *"Then I looked, and I heard the voice of many angels around the throne, the living creatures, and the elders; and the number of them was ten thousand times ten thousand, and thousands of thousands"* (Revelation 5:11).

Moving in for a closer look, one can immediately see that *"Around the throne were twenty-four thrones, and on the thrones I saw twenty-four elders sitting, clothed in white robes, and they had crowns of gold on their heads . . . Before the throne there was a sea of glass, like crystal"* (Revelation 4:4-6). The Bible speaks of Moses, and the elders of Israel, on Mt. Sinai. *"And they saw the God of Israel. And there was under His feet as it were a paved work of sapphire stone, and it was like the very heavens in its clarity"* (Exodus 24:10). Another place in Scripture refers to the sapphire stones as being "stones of fire." The sea of glass around the throne of God is huge, large enough for the saved and for untold thousands of angels as they worship Him.

Just as the priests and Levites served in the earthly sanctuary, those redeemed from this earth will be priests, and they will serve God in the New Jerusalem. John the Revelator states, *"and has made us kings and priests to His God and Father, to Him be glory and dominion forever and ever. Amen"* (Revelation 1:6). Again, the Bible states in 1 Peter 2:9, *"But you are a chosen generation, a royal priesthood, a holy nation. His own special people, that you may proclaim the praises of Him who called you out of darkness into His marvelous light."* The New Jerusalem and the new earth will become the center of God's Universe, and will become the eternal home of both God and man.

Because of Christ's gift of grace in sacrificing His life for the redemption of mankind, and the Holy Spirit's work of sanctification in the lives of the saved, the redeemed will be able to communicate the story of Salvation to the un-fallen universe as no other created beings can. As a result, they will be priests of God whose greatest joy will be to communicate the unfathomable depths of God's love to the un-fallen worlds. God's invitation is given to you and to me: *"come my children, enter into the joy of the Lord"*.

Just now, let each one of us commit or re-commit to accepting God's free gift of salvation, by grace, and through faith, in Jesus Christ; for *"how shall we escape if we neglect so great a salvation . . ."* (Hebrews 2:3).

DANIEL
PURE AND SIMPLE

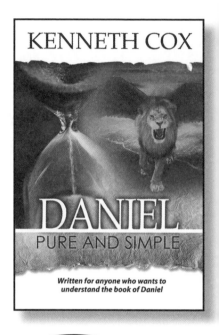

The books of Daniel and Revelation are companions. The prophecies given in Daniel are revealed further in Revelation, and fit together like a hand in a glove. As you understand the dreams and visions given to Daniel, you will find that John repeats the same prophecies and enlarges upon their meaning in Revelation. The book of Daniel is the first step in understanding Revelation. God gave these visions for guidance to His people, particularly in the closing events of time. He did not clothe them in mystery so they could not be understood, but by simply following Biblical principles, Daniel becomes Pure and Simple. It's written in an easy reading format, and as you progress through the book, the stories and prophecies will open up to give you understanding of God's love and His will for your life. The promise is given in Daniel 12:10 *"and none of the wicked shall understand, but the wise shall understand."*

REVELATION
PURE AND SIMPLE

This book on Revelation was not written for the theologian or Bible scholar. It was written for the man on the street—the man who's been told that Revelation is so full of symbolism that it cannot be understood. It was also written for those who have been told the events of Revelation have already passed and do not apply to us; that they will all take place in the future, long after we're gone; or that we will not be on earth when they take place—and a dozen other excuses for not understanding the truths that Jesus said we could and should.

It was written for the person who has a desire to know what Christ told John concerning the days we live in and for the person who wants to see the unfolding of prophecy, as one event after another takes place—each prophecy expanding and enlarging the next.

As you walk through Revelation, chapter by chapter in this easy reading format, your eyes will be opened to the roles played by different nations of the world.

Expect a blessing as you read, listen, and keep the things written in this book.

You can depend on it, for He promised it!

Written for anyone who wants to understand the book of Revelation

Price $14.95

To order:
Kenneth Cox Ministries
P.O. Box 1027
Loma Linda, CA 92354

951-232-9822

or at your local Adventist Book Center

3ABN
books

www.3abn.org

NOTES

NOTES

NOTES

NOTES

NOTES